FINANCIAL CITIZENSHIP

A volume in the series Cornell Global Perspectives

FINANCIAL CITIZENSHIP

Experts, Publics, and the Politics of Central Banking

ANNELISE RILES

Mario Einaudi Center for International Studies
Meridian 180
Cornell Global Perspectives Series

MARIO EINAUDI
Center *for* International Studies

CORNELL UNIVERSITY PRESS
ITHACA AND LONDON

First published 2018 by Cornell University Press

Printed in the United States of America

A catalog record of this book is available from the Library of Congress

978-1-5017-3272-0 paperback

978-1-5017-3273-7 epub/mobi

978-1-5017-3274-4 pdf

Contents

Financial Citizenship

Chapter 1

The Legitimacy of Central Banking

Government bailouts. Negative interest rates and markets that do not behave as economic models tell us they should. New populist and nationalist movements that target central banks and central bankers as a source of popular malaise. New regional organizations and geopolitical alignments laying claim to authority over the global economy. Bitcoin, cell phone banking, and other new forms of money and payment systems that challenge the authority of national currencies. Low confidence in conventional currencies and the state institutions behind them. Households, consumers, and workers facing increasingly intolerable levels of inequality. New risks associated with the financial health of pension funds. Public skepticism about the "science" of monetary policy and suspicion that central bankers serve the interests of a few at the expense of the rest. Malaise and unease among central bankers themselves about the limits of their tools and the double binds that define their work.

These dramatic conditions seem to cry out for new ways of understanding the purposes, roles, and challenges of central banks and financial governance more generally. The problem is not just that dominant economic models have failed to anticipate the current predicament. The problem is also that existing frameworks are far too narrow to take into account the broader political, social, and cultural implications of the work of central bankers on local, national, regional, and global scales. The unfinished agenda of the post-2008 reforms, arguably, is an intellectual one: how to understand the place of the state in the market and, in particular, the place of the central bank in relationship to politics—in all the senses of the term.

The problem is not just intellectual. It is also political. Over the past eight years, as central banks have grappled with financial crises and economic uncertainty, they have assumed new powers and also new responsibilities. This has opened up new legitimacy challenges. In many countries, central bankers are under attack from populist politicians who have come to power on the promise of bringing the central bank to heel. On the right and on the left, new civil society groups are challenging the idea that we should trust financial regulators because they are experts in governing the economy. They are challenging the notion—accepted by most for a generation—that *expertise confers legitimacy*. Various groups with vastly differing agendas are asking questions like: Do central banks have the power that they do, as a matter of law? Should they have that power, as a matter of policy? What are the proper roles of experts, elected officials, market participants, and the citizenry at large in stewarding national and global economies?

Central banks serve many important purposes in our national and global markets. First, they act as a clearinghouse between private banks. When you cash a check, your bank clears that check with your counterpart's bank through the central bank. This means that every bank has an account with the central bank. How much interest the central bank pays on funds in that account in turn affects how much interest banks can afford to pay their own depositors on their own accounts, or what interest rates banks will charge lenders. Second, central banks buy and sell government debt (and most recently other assets too, from stocks to real estate trusts) in order to stabilize the amount of money that is available in the market. If central banks buy lots of government bonds or stocks from banks in exchange for money, for example, the banks will have more cash on hand to loan to their customers. In theory, this should encourage banks to make more loans to more businesses, leading to more jobs.

Central banks also set rules for national banks as to how much money they must hold in reserve overnight. Different central banks have different mandates from their governments for all this monetary policy. Some are charged with focusing only on stabilizing prices—making sure that there is not too much inflation. Others are charged with focusing on other policy objectives, such as ensuring that there are enough jobs in the economy.

Central banks are also important regulators of banks. Their regulatory powers differ from country to country, but they often have the power to conduct inspections, audits, and other initiatives to ensure that banks' lending practices and reserves are sufficient that they will not pose a threat to the stability of the economy.

Finally, central banks play critical roles in calibrating the interface between national economies. They buy, sell, and store foreign currencies in a way that affects the value of the national currency relative to other currencies. Some central banks have agreements to loan one another currencies in times of crisis (so-called swap lines) on the understanding that a financial crisis in one national economy can quickly spread to another. Central banks cooperate to produce rules governing what banks in each country can do. This is done primarily through the Bank for International Settlements, a global organization of central banks, but also through other international institutions.

In this book I will show that the conflicts about who gets to decide how central banks do all these things, and about whether central banks are acting in everyone's interest when they do them—in short, conflicts over central bank legitimacy—are in large part the product of a *culture clash* between experts and the various global publics that have a stake in what central banks do. Experts—central bankers, regulators, market insiders, and their academic supporters—are a special community, a cultural group apart from many of the communities that make up the public at large. We are all products of our particular cultural environments. These cultures shape everything from our political views, to how we communicate, to what situations make us comfortable and uncomfortable. There is nothing inherently wrong with this, nor is one cultural view right or wrong. But when the gulf between the culture of those who govern and the cultures of the governed becomes unmanageable, the result is a legitimacy crisis. Legitimacy, in other words, is not just political. It is also cultural.

This book is a plea for all of us—experts and publics alike—to address this legitimacy crisis head on, for the sake of the health of both our economies and our democracies. It will not be easy. Central bankers and other experts will need to begin to anticipate and take into account the potential far-reaching political consequences of their policies. They will need to account for their roles in the rise of new populist movements angered by bank bailouts and foreign swap lines. And they will need to make much more intensive efforts to reach out beyond the boundaries of their own cultural community. Certain institutional reforms, and certain new uses of existing institutional levers, can facilitate this important work. Civil society institutions, from the press to the NGO community, have a critical role to play. And all of us as members of the public must engage the experts and the issues as if the things we value, from our retirements to our democratic process, depended on it.

If we do this, I will argue, we can put our institutions back on legitimate political ground. The purpose of public engagement is ultimately a *new theory and practice of legitimacy*, something other than "just trust us—we're the experts and we know best." We need a new explanation for why the work of central banks is important and legitimate that we can all believe in and a new way of living that legitimacy.

As an anthropologist and a legal scholar, I have spent the past twenty years studying the culture of central banking and the social relationships between financial regulators and other market participants. My method, as I have outlined elsewhere,[1] is ethnographic, the method traditionally deployed by anthropologists.[2] The core element of ethnography is fieldwork—a sustained and engaged form of study based on relations of trust with one's subjects, often over long periods of time. In my case, this has included field research within the financial markets, with financial policymakers, experts, and businesses across the world.

One of the reasons ethnography is so valuable to the study of finance is that the anthropologist specializes in understanding what is so important, so fundamental, so much a part of taken-for-granted agreed bases of social life that it goes largely unnoticed. If the actors could simply tell you about the symbolic structure underlying their kinship, for example, you wouldn't need ethnography; you could simply conduct a telephone survey. Long-term ethnography, moreover, gives me the opportunity for constant feedback and criticism from contacts in the market. When they think

I have gotten something wrong, they are not at all shy about letting me know.

This book is also the product of a collaborative effort by a group of academics, policymakers, and financial experts around the world to address the contradictions and limitations of the mainstream paradigm and to imagine an alternative. This work was organized and sponsored by Meridian 180, a nonpartisan global think tank of over 800 academics, policymakers, and businesspeople that I direct, based at Cornell Law School in partnership with Cornell University's Einaudi Center for International Studies, Ewha Womans University in Korea, The University of New South Wales in Australia, as well as the University of Tokyo Institute of Social Science, Ritsumeikan University, and Keio University in Japan. Over a five-year period, Meridian 180 organized a series of virtual and live discussions analyzing emerging trends and potential crises in central banking, from central bank independence to Bitcoin.

Several factors have distinguished our deliberations from many of the discussions in both academic and policy fields. First, unlike most conversations about central banking, our conversation has been deeply interdisciplinary and transprofessional. We have created a safe and respectful place in which experts can step out of their silos and explore other points of view. Second, given Meridian 180's focus on rethinking global questions from the point of view of a center of gravity in the Asia-Pacific region rather than the North Atlantic, our conversation has involved deep and rich participation from areas of the world that are usually only marginally represented in discussions of central banking. The Japanese experience with quantitative easing and other unconventional monetary policies known as "Abenomics"— policies that aim to fire up the economy by increasing the amount of money banks have available to lend to businesses and consumers and encouraging banks to make loans and consumers to invest in the stock market—has given the world one very important challenge to dominant paradigms of central banking. Through these experiences, the question of how to deal productively with the political dimension of central banking emerged as a theme for our collective deliberations.

In April 2016 and May 2017, a group of policymakers and academics convened at Cornell and in Brussels for a series of closed and off-the-record discussions. We analyzed various political dimensions of central banking. The meetings also included presentations by faculty and advanced doctoral students from the fields of law, political science, economics, sociology, and anthropology about the limits of the dominant paradigm, the state of the art, and what remains to be learned about the politics of central banking in various disciplines. Out of those discussions came the final argument of this book.

The book has three disparate audiences in mind—academics, policymakers, and the public at large. The ultimate message is the same for each, however—these three groups need to do much more listening, collaborating, and coordinating.

It Is Time for a Paradigm Shift in How We Think about Central Banks

A half century ago, the physicist Thomas Kuhn wrote about how a "paradigm"—a universally accepted framework for understanding how something works—changes. For example, how do people go from believing that the world is flat to believing that the world is round? People begin to notice that certain things cannot be explained by the dominant paradigm. At first, they deny those things—or explain them away. When that no longer becomes possible, they start to make exceptions or to suggest moderate amendments that preserve the core of the old paradigm while allowing for some change on the fringes. Finally, at some point, the cumulative weight of all those exceptions becomes so great that the dominant paradigm collapses. Often this is a tumultuous, chaotic moment: people don't know what to believe. Eventually a new paradigm emerges.

This same process is currently under way for how we understand what central banks do as an empirical matter, and what they should do as a normative matter. For some time, it had been commonly accepted that central bankers are technocratic experts, financial engineers whose work is removed from cultural considerations. We viewed managing the economy as something highly technical, with right and wrong answers, best left to the scientists. Just as with the process of engineering a bridge or building a rocket, without the proper training we would have little to add to the conversation, and probably little interest besides. We had no need to think about it too much, as we could trust the experts to come up with the right answers.

But events during and since the financial crisis of 2008 have rendered this understanding of central banks increasingly untenable, both to the experts and to the public at large. First, the economy is not responding as technical expertise says it should, leading to doubts about how good the expert knowledge is. Second, the public is beginning to realize that embedded in those highly technical questions are other issues that *are* of concern to ordinary people. Even if I as a layperson do not understand all the engineering that goes into building a bridge, I may care intensely about where that bridge does or does not get built and about how many lanes it has. To the extent that it determines how much of a toll I will have to pay every time I cross it, I will also care about what financing model is used to fund the construction. We are at a moment, in other words, at which the old paradigm is collapsing. But as of yet, there is no alternative understanding—no new paradigm—ready to take its place.

This book proposes a simple but transformative shift in our understanding of what central banks do, why they do it, and how they do it. Central bankers, like all policymakers, are cultural actors, and central banking is not just a technocratic but also a value-laden activity. This is nothing to be ashamed of, nothing illicit—on the contrary, it needs to be acknowledged, embraced, appreciated, studied, and also managed and stewarded. This basic insight gives us a new way of seeing what goes on in central banks and of evaluating the relationship between various actors in and around central banks, from academics to politicians, journalists, activists, and the average soccer mom voter. It also creates new responsibilities not just for central bankers but for the public and the institutions of civil society.

To say that central bankers are cultural actors or that value choices are at stake in the technical work of central banking is not to say that central bankers are *partisan* (favoring one political party or one candidate over another) or that they always or intentionally act in a way that favors one social, political, or economic group at the expense of another. Central bankers rightly bristle at that kind of simplistic attack, and, lacking a better explanation for their actions, retreat behind an equally caricatured public persona of the technocratic machine. We need a richer understanding of culture and value choices—as something ubiquitous, unavoidable, legitimate, important, highly complex, and entirely compatible with scientific and financial expertise.

Although the academic theories that guide central bank policymaking suggest that policy turns solely on economic factors, real-life central bankers navigate their way through dense cultural thickets on a daily basis. Existing academic theories and policy playbooks do not teach central bankers how to anticipate and manage the multiplex cultural environments in which they operate—from global to regional to domestic institutions, from populist media to government agencies and branches, from academic conferences and research projects to financial markets. The most successful central bankers learn to manage these daily pressures through apprenticeship to their seniors, or by trial and error.

Tensions and contradictions in the dominant story we tell about central banks only make the problem worse. For example, if central banking is a technocratic science, why do economies no longer respond to monetary policy as economic theories predict that they should? What exactly should be the purpose, mission, or mandate of the central bank vis-à-vis the nation or the global economy? How should the central bank be held accountable? Central bankers must respond to such questions all the time—from social movements, from journalists, from politicians, and even from judges.

Among ordinary citizens, consumers, and investors, the idea that central banking entails value choices and that values are culturally influenced is instinctively understood. But too often this value-ladenness becomes a reason to denounce the experts, and oversimplifications and misunderstandings abound. The financial crisis and the response of central banks and governments have created a new backlash among publics at large in many countries. These publics have lost faith in experts in general, and no longer believe that the game is fair. From currency disputes in the United States and China, to political conflicts over the fate of a common currency in Europe, to political movements such as Audit the Fed on the right and Occupy Wall Street on the left, many people outside the central bank no longer have faith in the idea that what central banks do is purely technocratic. Lacking a better understanding of the culture of central banking, citizens often denounce central bankers as politically partisan. Popular rage against financial policy will make future governmental and central bank intervention along the lines of what was done in 2008 all the more difficult. The anger and frustration in these debates speak to the need for a way of talking about central banking that can cross the cultural divide that separates experts from ordinary people. We need a new theory of central bank legitimacy that is both believable and worth believing in.

Chapter 2

The Challenge to the Technocracy

Central Bank Independence

The conventional framework for thinking about the legitimacy of central banks is a long-standing policy debate about central bank independence— How independent are central bankers from the political process? How independent should they be? Why is independence important and legitimate? And what combination of institutional arrangements or constraints best achieves competing goals of central bank independence and democratic governance?

For the past twenty to thirty years, many central banks in the developed world have set monetary policy more or less independently of formal political influence. This is a new state of affairs: in Japan, for example, the government only gave up direct political control over the Bank of Japan in 1997.[1] In many other countries, from Brazil to China, the central bank is not independent—it is an arm of the government. The consensus that central banks should be divorced from politics is relatively recent. Prior to the

1980s, only the United States, Germany, and Switzerland subscribed to any-thing resembling central bank independence. The original role of the central bank was highly integrated with the affairs of state governance: central banks provided liquidity to the banking system and financed government debt.[2] Where central banks are independent, although the heads of these central banks are chosen by elected leaders and confirmed by legislatures, their decisions are generally not subject to review by courts, and at least until re-cently it was deemed inappropriate for politicians to interfere with central bank business directly.

The political independence of the central bank, with its enormous power over the economy, is justified on grounds that monetary policy is more akin to science than to politics.[3] As Princeton professor and former vice chair of the Federal Reserve Alan Blinder argued in a recent lecture at Cornell, the nearly universal view since the late 1990s has been that central banking is primarily a technocratic activity that is purposely separated from the political process.[4]

The economic argument for separating central banking from politics is that the role of monetary policy is to modulate market trends. Independent central banks are supposed to act as a brake on spending when times are good by making borrowing more expensive, and to encourage spending when times are tough and people have lost confidence in the market by making borrowing cheaper. This kind of "countercyclical" activity is by definition out of sync with the mainstream thinking of the moment. But it is precisely the need for monetary policy to be out of sync with the main-stream that justifies central bank independence. Politicians are held ac-countable to the public on relatively short election cycles. But central bankers should have longer time horizons, and for this they must be insulated from the political process.

The establishment of central bank independence "sounds like, in some ways, a right wing coup," said Adam Posen in a lecture at Cornell Univer-sity. "In many ways it actually was. But it was presented by the economics profession as straight up, Pareto optimization. . . . This over excess of de-mocracy pushing for inflation made everybody worse off, and . . . in the end [by insulating central banks from the democratic process] you weren't saving one group versus another. What you were doing was just getting the whole society to be more patient and everyone would be better off in the end."[5] A 1993 paper by Alberto Alesina and Lawrence Summers provides a typical example of this view of central banks as a check on the excesses of democracy.[6] Using data from various countries, the authors examine the correlation between average inflation rates and the degree of central bank independence. They find that countries with more independent central banks have lower levels of inflation—presumably because central bankers have the autonomy to adhere to monetary policies that are unpopular in the short run.

Working on the assumption that the goal is to root out politics from central banking, political scientists have dedicated themselves to defining the political conditions that produce central bank independence from politics. As Erin Lockwood explains in her survey of the literature on the politics of central banking, the main focus of political scientists during the 1990s and 2000s was on calculating degrees of central bank independence. The "main assumption" driving this focus was that "central bank independence bolsters the credibility of low-inflation commitments, given economic actors' rational expectations of defection from these commitments in the face of electoral incentives."[7]

Despite the apparent correlation between independence and low inflation, many scholars now doubt the claim that central bank independence necessarily leads to low inflation. Research by Adam Posen actually finds that the causation goes the other way: independence does not predict inflation levels—rather, low inflation levels lead to central bank independence.[8] Moreover, in an era in which inflation is almost nonexistent in developed economies, curbing inflation is no longer an adequate rationale for central banks' independence in those economies.[9]

Even among proponents of central bank independence, the rationale for independent central banks and the breadth of powers they should have are contested. Should these powers be limited to inflation-targeting monetary policy through government bond purchases? Or should an independent central bank have the power to buy and sell other kinds of debt and assets? And should legislators give central banks a very clear and narrowly focused mandate to guide their actions, or should they instead be given discretion to manage different goals such as full employment and low inflation that may sometimes be in tension with one another? The situation gets even more complicated given that there are different explanations for why a central bank buys or sells assets in the financial market. We can interpret these actions as merely aimed at stabilizing interest rates, something traditionally within the authority of the central bank. Or we can interpret these actions as aimed at ensuring the wider financial stability of the national—or global—economy, something that is more traditionally the responsibility of the political branches of government.

Moreover, central banks do many things other than monetary policy, including important regulatory and supervision work, both domestically and internationally. Should the central bank's power be limited to monetary policy? Or should it also have powers to monitor or regulate market participants? Different central banks around the world have different authorities and responsibilities, especially in the area of regulation.

A further challenge is that central banks' mandates are defined in terms of domestic economies. But financial markets are deeply interconnected, such that a problem in one place impacts another. We learned in the last financial crisis how the impact of something as local as bad loans in the U.S. housing market had repercussions for the livelihoods of people in far-flung parts of the world who were in no way "responsible" for the results. Our actions and political choices have consequences—and often adverse consequences—for people who live in faraway places we will never even visit. Likewise, our economic rights and obligations are shaped by international agreements and policies that are very distant from our local politician's office. It is impossible to disentangle the global economy. Our economic fates are intertwined. Our options and standard of living are shaped by economic events elsewhere. For this reason, our choices need to take into account these wider effects and relationships.

Central banks are charged with the welfare of their own national economies and have no explicit mandate to take into account the suboptimal impacts of their policies on other economies.[10] While central bankers are keenly aware of the possible conflict between domestic interests and global interests, and many appreciate that fulfilling their mandate to stabilize the domestic economy necessitates concern for the stability of the global economy as well, they are politically bound to prioritize domestic interests.

The important point for our purposes, however, is that regardless of the position one takes on these questions, central bank legitimacy turns on central bankers being a *community apart*. If central bankers are too close to politicians or the public, it is assumed that they are not doing their job. Yet even the strongest advocates of central bank independence recognize that the rule of the market by a handful of experts is something that somehow needs to be squared with democratic commitments to governance by the people through elected representatives.[11] There is a trade-off here: the public (through its elected representatives) voluntarily gives up political control in order to get the benefit of rule by experts.

How to manage this trade-off? Communication, or "central bank transparency," is the mainstream answer. Communication addresses the problem of the central bank's political legitimacy by treating its authority as delegated from the public. As Alan Blinder puts it, "In exchange for its broad grant of authority, the central bank owes the public transparency and accountability."[12]

Yet central banks are not entirely independent from the political process. The governors of central banks are typically appointed by the executive and must report frequently to legislatures. Moreover, as Blinder points out, unless central bank independence is mandated constitutionally (as is the case in the European Union, where it is enshrined in the Maastricht Treaty), independence can always be revoked by the legislature through the same simple process used to revise a law.

Any successful central banker knows that doing one's job well entails navigating multiple layers of national politics—from battles with elected officials, to conflict among government divisions (a classic one of these being the perennial conflict between the Treasury, or the Ministry of Finance and the Central Bank). Managing this kind of politics is simply part of a day's work at everything but the lowest echelon. From this point of view, a model of central banking premised entirely on political independence tells you little, at best, about how to go about doing your daily work. At worst, this model makes you feel like you must be doing something wrong, as though, as Adam Posen puts it, "you're going to have to get your hands dirty."[13] Could we imagine a way of thinking about what central banks do, a vocabulary and set of analytical tools for evaluating decisions, that would not leave this necessary, and indeed, important work, out of the picture?

The extraordinary actions taken by central banks in the context of the financial crisis raised questions, in the eye of the public, about central banks' independence from governments and hence from the influence of interest groups that capture the political process.[14] In the United States, for example, the close (and highly effective) coordination between the Federal Reserve and the Treasury Department during the crisis—and, indeed, the lengths to which Fed and Treasury officials went to portray a united front—had the collateral effect of shattering the image of the central bank as independent from the government.

If central banks are not, in fact, independent in times of crisis, can we speak of them as truly independent in ordinary times? Although some may wish to draw a clean line between how they justify their actions in ordinary times and in crisis times, as former deputy governor of the Bank of England Paul Tucker points out, it is in fact difficult to distinguish "peacetime" and "wartime."[15] The actions in each period shape the other—and so it makes more sense to think about the central bank's role more globally.

The general story that central banks are divorced from the political process has a dangerous political consequence: when it is discovered (by the public, or by politicians, or indeed by insiders themselves) that central banks must engage in activities associated with the political process—that they don't have "clean hands"—then central banks are opened up to criticism. It seems they have done something wrong. The public feels betrayed. Politicians seize on the contradiction between the story we tell about central banks and the reality of what central banks must (and indeed, should) do, to score political points by attacking bureaucratic "elites." Central bankers themselves feel that they are failing to live up to their charge. The public story—which sophisticated insiders always knew to be incomplete at best—causes unnecessary damage.

From here, it is only a small step for some academics, politicians, and members of the electorate to ask why central banks should be independent from the political process in the first place. As Marcelo Prates points out, legislatures have responded to the collapse of faith in the independence of central banks postcrisis by paying greater attention to the oversight of central banks than before.[16] Add to this also the increase in lawsuits against central banks. Most recently, the European Court of Justice (ECJ) has reaffirmed the authority of the European Central Bank in matters of monetary policy, and the judgment of the ECJ in turn squeaked by in the German high court. But whether courts will continue to back central bank independence in light of the restlessness of the public remains to be seen.

The Japanese Example: Abenomics

This question—Why should central banks be independent?—got an early hearing in Japanese prime minister Shinzo Abe's 2012 campaign for office. The word "Abenomics" first appeared in the financial press during this campaign. It referred to Abe's promise to force the Bank of Japan to undertake unconventional monetary policies to spur the economy out of its decades-long stagnation. Many central bankers reacted with dismay at Abe's willingness to thumb his nose at central bank independence and his promise to bring the central bank under his political control. Yet many financial market participants and citizens felt that the ends justified the means.

Almost five years after its launch in 2012, Abenomics has largely failed as an economic strategy. Haruhiko Kuroda, the governor of the Bank of Japan who was appointed by Abe to implement Abenomics, was not able to lift the nation's economy out of its long-standing stagnation—interest rates remain more or less where they were at the launch of Abenomics. But as a political project, Abenomics has been highly successful. Abe's political party has repeatedly won elections by landslide votes since Abenomics began. And beyond the narrow question of Abe's own political future, Kuroda's interventions in the market have had, arguably, a larger cultural impact on Japan. Abe was elected on the heels of the Fukushima disasters, in the midst of Japan's never-ending "lost decades," a time in which Japanese people's confidence in the future and hope for themselves and their society were at an all-time low. For many, it was exciting to see something finally happening, to see Japan as a society turning a corner, taking a chance on a new approach.

Kuroda's policies arguably rendered palatable a nationalist politics that most Japanese said they found distasteful. As long as Abe was getting economic results, people seemed willing to put up with political views and policies out of line with the mainstream, from changes to public school textbooks' accounts of World War II to laws that limit freedom of the press. Although Abenomics failed in its goal of achieving two percent inflation within two years, it has translated into political results for Abe and his right-wing political coalition. For better or worse, this cultural and political effect of Abenomics is a highly significant consequence of central bank policy.

The U.S. Example: Trump, Occupy Wall Street, and End the Fed

In the run-up to the U.S. presidential election of 2016, central banking became a key theme. In January 2016, legislation proposed by libertarian senator Rand Paul and cosponsored by presidential candidates Marco Rubio and Ted Cruz on the right and Bernie Sanders on the left, passed in the House of Representatives before being narrowly defeated in the Senate.[17] The bill, known as Audit the Fed (H.R. 24/S. 264), aimed to eliminate the secrecy surrounding Federal Reserve deliberations and to allow Congress to review Fed monetary policy decisions. This bill proposed to do this by allowing "the [Government Accountability Office (GAO)] to view all materials and transcripts related to a meeting of the Fed's Federal Open Market Committee (FOMC) at essentially any time and require the GAO, at Congressional request, to provide recommendations on monetary policy, including potentially on individual FOMC interest-rate decisions."[18]

The Audit the Fed debate raised several disparate concerns about central banking. For libertarians such as Paul, the key issue was liberty. They were concerned in particular by the encroaching power of an executive branch of government that they believed was manipulating the Fed from behind the scenes. In an op-ed, Paul and his adviser Mark Spitznagel wrote that the bill, "if passed, would bring to an end to the Federal Reserve's unchecked— and even arguably unconstitutional—power in the financial markets and the economy."[19] Invoking the neoliberal economist Ludwig von Mises, they argued that the key issue is political—"a matter of liberty, not merely economics."[20]

Beyond the libertarian point about the dangers of unrepresentative government, proponents of Audit the Fed on both the right and the left pointed to a cultural issue: the close personal relationship between individual Fed officials and Wall Street executives. Critics of the Federal Reserve have often intimated that this close relationship leads to policies that benefit Wall Street at the expense of ordinary people. Paul and Spitznagel seized on these social ties—"the revolving door from Wall Street to the Treasury to the Fed and back again"—as a cultural explanation for their political critique of Fed policy: "The Fed is, indeed, a political, oligarchic force, and a key part of what looks and functions like a banking cartel. During the 2007–08 financial crisis, the Fed's true nature was clear to anyone paying attention. As the Treasury began bailing out the investment banks from the consequences of their profligate risk-taking (and in some cases fraudulent schemes), the Fed moved in tandem, further purchasing the underwater assets of these institutions, as well as actually paying interest to the commercial banks (hemorrhaging from risky loans) for reserves they kept parked at the Fed."[21]

Bernie Sanders agreed: "Unfortunately, an institution that was created to serve all Americans has been hijacked by the very bankers it regulates."[22] He raised concerns about conflicts of interest in bank chief executives serving on Fed boards. "These are clear conflicts of interest, the kind that would not be allowed at other agencies. We would not tolerate the head of Exxon Mobil running the Environmental Protection Agency. We don't allow the Federal Communications Commission to be dominated by Verizon executives. And we should not allow big bank executives to serve on the boards of the main agency in charge of regulating financial institutions."[23]

In addition to the provisions in the Audit the Fed bill, Sanders proposed that all board members be nominated by the president and confirmed by the Senate. The goal, he stated, was "making the Federal Reserve a more democratic institution, one that is responsive to the needs of ordinary Americans rather than the billionaires on Wall Street."[24]

Fed officials and their defenders largely ducked the cultural question altogether. Mostly, they asserted that these proposals were unworkable. Janet Yellen asserted that the bill "would politicize monetary policy and it would bring short-term political pressures to bear on the Fed."[25] In an influential blog post, Ben Bernanke emphasized the "technical" nature of central banking: "Congress is not well-suited to make monetary policy decisions itself, because of the technical and time-sensitive nature of those decisions. Moreover, both historical experience and formal studies . . . have shown that monetary policy achieves better results when central bankers are allowed to focus on the longer-term interests of the economy, free of short-term political considerations."[26]

Larry Summers, interestingly, accepted Bernie Sanders's cultural critique: "Sanders is right that Fed governance has been and is overly tied up with the financial sector. Each of the 12 regional Feds has a board of directors that is made up of nine people—three banking representatives, three private-sector non-banking representatives and three public interest representatives. The fact that a member of Goldman Sachs's board at the time of the 2008 crisis was the 'public interest' chairman of the New York Fed board is, to put it mildly, indefensible."[27]

Yet he went on to reject the idea of requiring congressional approval as unworkable on two further cultural grounds. First, he argued that the culture of Congress itself is dysfunctional, and hence Congress is not well suited to represent the people effectively in regulating the Federal Reserve.

He also pointed out that many other important government bodies meet in private and do not have to release their meeting minutes. Second, he implicitly argued for the *benefits* of a tight-knit culture of regulators and financial executives in suggesting that having industry leaders as senior officials at the Fed is not necessarily a bad thing. As Summers put it, "There is a tension between acquiring expertise and avoiding co-optation or cognitive capture."[28]

In the context of the 2016 political campaign, however, these debates morphed into a simpler and cruder set of political accusations. The claim was that Fed officials were playing partisan politics—that they were supporting Democrats in their election bids against Republicans because of close personal relationships between Fed officials and members of the "Democratic elite." Janet Yellen was called before Congress to answer for the conflict of interest some senators saw in Fed officials donating private funds to Hillary Clinton's political campaign.[29] Donald Trump, the Republican presidential nominee, accused Janet Yellen of purposely keeping interest rates low so that the economy would be booming at the time of the election and hence make voters feel satisfied with the status quo and stick with Democrats. In his assertion that Yellen "should be ashamed of herself," he insinuated collusion between the Fed and the executive on the basis of personal relationships: "She's obviously political and doing what Obama wants her to do."

The response of Fed officials to this particular accusation was swift and total denial. "Partisan politics plays no role in our decisions," Yellen asserted. "We do not discuss politics at our meetings and we do not take politics into account in our decisions," she said.[30] Minneapolis Fed president Neel Kashkari echoed this sentiment, stating that in policy deliberations at the U.S. central bank, "politics does not play a part, I can assure you of that."[31]

For her part, Democratic presidential nominee Hillary Clinton played the expert card, arguing that Trump's accusations were unsophisticated and dangerous: "Words have consequences. Words move markets. Words can be misinterpreted. Words can have effects on people's 401(k)'s, their pension funds, their stock portfolios. [Mr. Trump] should not be adding the Fed onto his long list of institutions and individuals that he is maligning."[32]

Yet in matters of culture, the senators were arguably a bit more expert than the central bankers. Scott Garrett, Republican congressman from New

Jersey, put it as follows: "As the saying goes, perception is reality. Whether you like it or not, the public increasingly believes that Fed independence is nothing more than a myth."[33]

From Independence to Interdependence

For better or worse, the era in which central banks were entrusted with acting with little interference from the public or elected officials is probably over. "When I first worked at the Federal Reserve," Alan Blinder joked in a lecture at Cornell University, "most members of the public probably thought that [the Federal Reserve] was a forest somewhere."[34] This is most definitely no longer the case. Central banks are now subject to increasingly stringent legislative oversight as legislators make growing demands for reporting on central bank policies, set the targets for those policies, and even float proposals to subject the specific policies central banks pursue to legislative review. We seem to be entering a new era in which more muscular executive branches feel no compunction about criticizing the central bank or its officials, or about expressing their own policy preferences clearly and directly.

What can or should policymakers do with or about the decline of political independence? Existing academic theories and policy playbooks do not teach central bankers how to anticipate and navigate the new political environment in which they now operate. These theories do not give policymakers, market participants, and the public at large the tools they need to productively define the issues and debate what should be done about them.

The old and perhaps still dominant approach would be to mimic the ostrich with its head in the sand—to simply ignore the situation or deny its existence completely; hoping the entire problem of the central bank's political legitimacy will go away. Such, arguably, was the approach of Federal Reserve officials to President Trump's attacks during the 2016 presidential election. This, of course, only succeeds in enraging the public and tipping the hand of demagogues.

A second and equally dangerous course of action is the exact reverse of the first. Faced with the overt politicization of central bank activities by governments and political movements, some central bankers may choose simply to cave to politics—to embrace or at least accept the overt politicization of finance by nationalist leaders. Such is, arguably, the approach of Governor Haruhiko Kuroda of the Bank of Japan.

In the aftermath of the 2008 crisis, a number of other proposals have been made for increasing central banks' accountability to elected officials and for increasing the transparency of internal decision-making processes. For example, some have suggested that central banks are akin to administrative agencies, and hence that we can find models for political accountability in the experience with other administrative agencies such as the Environmental Protection Agency or the Fair Trade Commission.[35] Law professor Adam Levitin argues for the necessity of some kind of legal structure that would set competing political interests against one another in order to "neutralize" them.[36] Yet these are not the only possible responses to the attack on central bank independence. The legitimacy of central banking involves much more than formal legal independence or institutional fixes on purported "capture" by special interest groups (such as banks).[37]

Empirical evidence already demonstrates that legal guarantees of independence do not in fact suffice—there are many cases in which a central bank has legal autonomy and yet in practice there is substantial involvement of the government in policymaking. Rather, the evidence shows that the kinds of contacts and informal arrangements between various units of the central bank, from the research department to the foreign affairs department, and also the circulation of personnel between central banks and government offices—cultural and social factors—are better indices of actual independence.[38]

How might one respond productively to attacks on central bank independence? One of the fundamental problems with the claim that central banking is technocratic work set apart from what happens in government, the market, or public life, and therefore not shaped by value judgments, is that it does not correspond to how either ordinary people or experts experience the issues. Because the decisions, choices, and personal networks of central bankers are already deeply intertwined with the political process, we need a new explanation of the purposes of central banking, and a new way of evaluating what central banks do. We need a story that fosters a richer conversation about political legitimacy—about how to reconcile the need for expert knowledge in financial regulation and policy with the democratic challenge to expert authority. We need a story that fits current realities, one that the citizenry can truly believe in.

We might begin with some introspection about how central bank independence became the holy grail of central bank legitimacy. As we saw, the (contested) rationale is that independence leads to lower inflation. Yet, as Jonathan Kirshner observes, the economic evidence supporting the notion that low inflation should be the ultimate macroeconomic goal is at best "modest and ambiguous."[39] Modest inflation can be a good thing, not a bad thing—in fact, in today's deflationary era it is now the goal of most central bank policies.

If the dominant justifications for central bank independence do not make strong economic sense, perhaps they tell us more about the culture of central bankers, and about the wider economic culture in which they operate, than about economics.[40] We will explore this culture in the next chapter.

When we speak of independence, *from whom* do we imagine that central banks are independent, anyway? The discussion has mostly focused on independence from government, but, as Adam Posen argues, central banks are certainly not independent from the leaders of the financial markets. Their political authority and independence from other branches of government turn on support from the financial sector, and they cannot engage in policymaking without this support.[41] Legal scholar Peter Conti-Brown likewise proposes that the very term "independence" is misleading because it deflects attention from "a broader, more explanatory context where Fed insiders and interested outsiders form relationships using law and other tools to implement a wide variety of specific policies."[42]

A better way to think about central banks, therefore, is to see them not as independent but as *interdependent* actors in the economic and political spheres. Interdependence suggests that legitimacy comes from a different place—it comes from productive and principled collaboration, not from autonomy. Legitimacy, from this point of view, is a matter of cultural ideas and social relations as much as it is a matter of legal authority. Our ultimate goal should be legitimacy in the context of the cultural environment, not independence for its own sake. In the chapters ahead, we will explore the contours of collaborative legitimacy and how it can be achieved.

Chapter 3

The Culture of Central Banking

A Definition of Culture

The very idea of a culture of central banking may sound odd because central bankers are experts, and we imagine that experts are (or at least should be) unbiased, detached, and set apart from the wider culture. But for exactly this reason, central bankers, regulators, market insiders, and their academic supporters are a special community, a cultural group apart from many of the communities that make up the public at large. "I feel more comfortable with other central bankers around the world than I do with ordinary Japanese people," one senior Bank of Japan official once told me. The same is true on the other side of the divide. "Isn't it boring talking to those people?" my Japanese hairstylist asked me when I explained my research at the Bank of Japan.

Before we can see how central banking is in fact cultural, we need to say what we mean by culture. Culture is the ensemble of collectively held values, beliefs, commitments, and general ways of doing things. It includes everything from how we dress to what we believe. Anthropology is the social science devoted to the study of culture. Two generations ago, the renowned anthropologist Clifford Geertz defined culture as "a system of inherited conceptions expressed in symbolic forms by means of which men communicate, perpetuate, and develop their knowledge about and attitudes toward life."[1] Culture in this sense is shaped and experienced by the institutions in which we live, grow up, are trained, and work. Culture therefore is a product of history, and also of economics. But since it shapes what human beings believe and therefore what they do, culture also shapes history and economics.

The starting point of a modern study of culture is an appreciation that what looks irrational or even reprehensible in one context or from one point of view looks perfectly rational and even admirable from another.[2] Any science of culture therefore must seek to understand other people's way of knowing the world, on their own terms, before passing judgment on them. Our goal therefore is to understand the culture of central banking, how it came to be, and what actions and thoughts are possible for someone who is part of this culture, not to criticize. This is a perspective that allows us to shed new light on the challenges of central banking, as well as on how we—experts and publics—might respond to these challenges.

Anthropologists also know that although we are all heavily influenced by our culture, cultures do not dictate our thinking or moral choices. In every culture, people interpret shared cultural values differently and make different ethical or strategic decisions. There is always plenty of room for agency, choice, and change in any community. This also means that cultures are internally divided and that values are always contested. People offend each other, wrong each other, misunderstand each other, exert power over each other, and leverage the tensions and ambiguities in cultural norms in order to push for changes in those norms. Just because there is such a thing as a culture of central banking does not mean that all central bankers think alike. On the contrary, there is plenty of conflict within central banks, and these disputes are an important part of the culture.

It is also well established that cultures are not like billiard balls—that there are no "pure" cultures untouched by other cultures.[3] Rather, cultures are hybrid, overlapping and constantly mixing and combining into dynamic new forms. Forces from markets to education to migration to popular culture ensure that all of us participate in multiple cultures at once. So central bankers are not in fact cut off from the world—they have a foot in other worlds and bring those cultural influences into the central bank.

All this is why culture is never a fixed and given thing.[4] It is constantly changing as it is translated to new audiences and adapts to cultural influences from outside. Hence any assertions about the "real" cultural values of a given society are necessarily ideological or political claims rather than truth. The culture of central banking fifty or ten years ago bore some important relationship to today's but also differed in significant ways.

One important aspect of any culture is how it represents itself to the outside world. What "the community" and its values are is partly a product of their representation in speeches, blog posts, regulations, doctrines, and documents.[5] This brings us to something anthropologists call "reflexivity." It is now universally acknowledged that the "facts" of culture are not, as we imagine the laws of physics, "out there" to be discovered; rather they are produced in the experience of people describing themselves to others and also in the experience of dialogue, confrontation, or mutual learning that characterizes cultural research.[6] And yet the difficulties in knowing the "truth" of culture—indeed, the fact that there is no singular truth to know, that culture is not so much an object as an endless process of translation—do not relieve us of the burden to try to understand and know.

In *The Invention of Culture*, Roy Wagner argues that the study of culture involves a relationship between two sets of cultural values. "The understanding of another culture involves the relationship between two varieties of the human phenomenon; it aims at the creation of an intellectual relation between them, an understanding that includes both of them."[7] Culture is not a thing out there, like a rabbit or a carrot,[8] but rather a heuristic. It is a tool for translating one set of meanings into another, for "drawing self-knowledge from the understanding of others and vice-versa."[9] This formulation of culture challenges us to engage in a collaborative experiment.[10] This does not undermine the scientific nature of the inquiry; rather, it humanizes it.

So when we speak of the culture of central banking, we are actually engaging in a creative and difficult dialogue across the boundary that separates experts and the public. Culture here is a tool for a new kind of relationship between the two.

The Culture of Central Banking

Central banks are not machines—they are cultural institutions. That is, they are collections of human beings, with all of the tensions, biases, disagreements, uncertainties, common aspirations, career trajectories, and ideological orientations that define any other group of human beings. As Peter Conti-Brown puts it, "The Federal Reserve is a 'They,' not an 'It.'"[11] This also means that central bankers are not machines—they have biases and blind spots, cultural particularities and preferences, like everyone else.

To understand the culture of central banking we need to focus in on the social dimensions of the central bank as an institution. This includes how people are recruited, how they are trained, how they are promoted, and where they go when they leave the central bank. For example, Japanese central bankers are still predominantly recruited right out of university or graduate school and then are put through an elaborate multiyear training and promotion program. This usually involves spending extensive time at branch offices outside of Tokyo where they are sent out to talk to local bankers and merchants. This experience is critical because it gives them some exposure to the real economy. They usually spend their entire careers at the central bank and retire to positions as part- or full-time college lecturers or as advisers to industry. There is relatively little career pressure to make friends in industry, therefore, because central bankers are not beholden to the private sector for their immediate future.

The culture of central banking also includes the daily practices and rituals of the institution—what people do every day, the internal rules and expectations, and also the important ceremonial events in the life of the institution. For example, formal dress codes and subtle gradations on those codes may define internal hierarchies. The usual dress code in most central banks involves conservative suits—ideally not too flashy or expensive. One American central banker once joked to me that if your shoes are too fancy people will wonder where you got the money from. In this understanding, the subtleties of the dress code expressed central bankers' financial independence from market participants.

In Japan, for many years, women wore company uniforms, whereas men wore clothes of their own choosing—until female employees convinced superiors that this cultural practice marked women as different and unequal. In the summer months, employees skip the jacket and tie, and the buildings go with minimal air conditioning. But at the Bank of Japan at the time of my research, this policy still did not apply to women—women still had to dress up exactly as before in the sweltering heat.

These practices may seem trivial, but they tell us something important about how people live their roles and their work day to day. They also shape policy. As I have written about elsewhere,[12] the Bank of Japan has its own distinct way of managing and gathering information about market participants, and providing guidance that is highly effective in Japan, but different from what goes on in New York or London.

There are also special moments—public speeches, academic conferences, promotion ceremonies, special meetings. All of these events, and the preparation that goes into making them happen, shape people's thinking and provide opportunities for turf wars as well as for solidarity. They can also become platforms for engaging with the outside world. The way these events unfold is a product of the specific history of the central bank in question and reflects its own specific culture. Adam Posen gives the example of simple but consequential differences in the way policy committee meetings take place in the United States and in England, two countries with similar ideologies, markets, and even traditions.[13]

But central bankers are also products of their larger cultural environment. Their ways of thinking, of making decisions, of building relationships, or of engaging in conflict with market participants, with other government institutions, with the public, and with other central banks around the world, are shaped by the cultures that have formed them. As institutions, central banks are also shaped by the history and culture around them.

There is significant variation in the political, cultural, intellectual, and economic environments in which central banks operate. Although there are important similarities, the cultures of central banking in the United States, the United Kingdom, and Japan, for example—not to mention in China or Malaysia—are profoundly different. Even the pathways by which the central bank is connected to the public and to the political branches of government are different. For instance, in China, where most large financial institutions are state owned, the relationship between the central bank and the market has a very different character.[14] These differences can in turn generate disagreements at the regional and international level about how the global economy should be managed and also result in different local outcomes for the same global policies.[15]

At a Meridian 180 conference, there was a lively discussion among current and former central bankers of the subtle but powerful cultural barriers to developing countries' full participation in G20 meetings. Agendas are often set and important decisions are often made in informal social settings on the sidelines of formal proceedings. These settings are accessible only to persons of certain cultural backgrounds. A central banker from the developing world described how the night before the formal meetings European and American central bankers often meet at a private club to socialize. This central banker pointed out that key decisions were made at those social events, and he complained that central bankers from his country could not participate in those discussions. A European central banker responded that his critic's countrymen should just learn the rules of the private club world so that they can join those parties. He pointed to Japanese colleagues as models of cultural outsiders who were literally part of the club because, he said, they knew how to behave in those settings. Such an exchange tells us much about how culture frames a politics of inclusion of some and exclusion of others according to unwritten norms and practices.

It is important to emphasize that there is no eliminating culture. There is no such thing as a culture-free bureaucracy. Rather, once we recognize that bureaucrats—like everyone else—are socially situated, we open up new possibilities for collaboration and coordination (as well as competition) with other social actors. This can help us to achieve specific policy goals and address possible biases. Yet we first need to recognize our cultural embeddedness, as both a strength and a weakness, but, in any case, as a reality.

Beyond this, there are also the more specific social relations that central bankers maintain with their counterparts in the financial sector. Central bankers share a similar educational background (and even classmate ties) with many elite financial market participants. They speak the same language and feel comfortable together. They meet often in formal and informal settings—from private clubs to dinner parties to classmate reunions—and know one another as friends. In those settings they talk about their work and often come to share certain given assumptions about the economy, the financial markets, and the directions policy should take.

Of course, the social dimension of central banking has advantages and important policy uses too. Elsewhere, I have suggested that, empirically speaking, relations between central bankers and financial market participants represent an important source of central bank legitimacy.[16] These relationships are important sources of information and important vehicles for implementing central bank policy. They can be called upon to shift the narrative when central banks are under attack. The most skilled central bankers have learned to make use of these relations to get their job done—whether it is gathering information about market conditions or cajoling market participants to accept certain policy directions. Yet there is no policy playbook, no script, that teaches policymakers how to handle their status as social actors embroiled in real social institutions. The policy manuals proceed as if technocrats act outside of the web of connections that, in fact, define their thoughts and actions.

In most cases, it is the cultural effects of these social relations, rather than actual quid pro quos, that result in what many outsiders see as central banks' favoritism toward large financial institutions. As discussed further later, an important implication of acknowledging this kind of cultural politics is that central bankers must widen their networks and engage with a much broader range of market participants and citizens. We need to expand the range of constituencies to whom central banks are "culturally accountable," in informal terms, for their legitimacy.

The Power of Ideas

As Peter Katzenstein explains, conceptual "conventions are shared social templates, 'often tacit but also conscious, that organize and coordinate actions in predictable ways,'" and that serve as "agreed-upon, if flexible, guides for economic interpretation and interaction."[17] All expert communities—professions, schools, and disciplines—define themselves by the way they set boundaries around ways of knowing things. In the field of central banking, certain economics departments dominate as key training sites—places where ideas are taught, where a specific language for thinking about the economy is learned, where the common sense is imparted from one generation to the next.

Sociologists Yves Dezalay and Bryant Garth have described the impact of those training sites on economic policy. They talk of how young economists from the developing world came to the University of Chicago, Harvard, and elsewhere to learn the "science" of economics and went home with very particular (and, the authors argue, skewed) policy prescriptions.[18] A similar story could be told about the training of central bankers around the world. Elite central bankers are, on the whole, graduates of a few key economics departments. They are specialists in only one discipline. Moreover, as Katharina Pistor points out, the economic training at these institutions ignores much of the discipline's own tradition of doubt about the self-regulatory and self-sustaining capacities of markets.

Gillian Tett has coined a phrase for the problem: silo thinking.[19] As Tett argues, prior to the 2008 crisis (and still, unfortunately, to this day) experts lived in their own knowledge silos—worlds in which most everyone thought like them. Silos are not necessarily all bad. In fact, they are necessary. One of the features of expertise is that it must exclude certain other forms of knowledge in order to define its own parameters. The very nature of expertise—what enables it to do its work—is the limit it places on one's ways of knowing a given object.[20] Silos shut out certain kinds of "noise" so that other patterns can be grasped.

Yet this means that every kind of expertise has its blind spots—areas that are not germane to that form of expert knowledge.[21] The result is that policies often reflect the specific blind spots of the expertise on which they are built.[22] The best experts know this—they are acutely aware of what they do not know, cannot explain, or are likely to miss given their own methodologies. Yet when expertise gets so all-encompassing that experts are not able to communicate with, or learn from, other ways of seeing the world, experts lose awareness of those blind spots. Science turns into dogma. The result is one particular conceptual template for understanding the economy, one way for identifying problems and crafting solutions.

This can be all the more problematic as expertise is shared across different contexts—when central bankers from one jurisdiction borrow the tools of central bankers in another, for example. One of the hallmarks of expertise is a certain "cut and paste" approach—models, language, tools, or routines developed in one context are transplanted by the expert to another context. Preparedness drills for nuclear war are repurposed as preparedness drills for bio threats. Economic programs developed for the United States are transposed to Latin America.[23] Payments technologies developed by a central bank in a highly developed economy are adopted by a central bank in a developing economy. This allows for dramatic economies of scale, but it also increases the impact of blind spots as the premises, purposes, and background knowledge behind programs is lost in the transplantation, and as projects developed for one context are repurposed for a very different one.

As political philosophers, philosophers of science, and anthropologists have shown, certain ideas make certain kinds of facts "thinkable." Without an appropriate conceptual box to put it in, a piece of information can become heretical (Copernicus's assertion that the Earth rotated around the Sun, for example) or, worse yet, entirely nonsensical. This is what the political philosopher Antonio Gramsci meant when he spoke of ideas as "hegemonic"—the power of the idea to become so commonsensical, so generally accepted, that it does not even deserve notice, let alone criticism.[24] When an idea becomes hegemonic, any contrary idea or any fact that does not fit in the dominant idea is apprehended as pure craziness. For example, the historian Liaquat Ahamed shows that central bankers during the interwar period were prisoners of their belief in a particular economic orthodoxy. Their conviction that sound monetary management depended on the gold standard kept them from pursuing policy options that might have prevented the Great Depression.[25]

In central banking, the conventions that have dominated in recent years are neoclassical economic theories. These conventions define the issues for policymaking and the zone for political compromise. We now know that these conventions have serious limitations. As Joseph Stiglitz argues, the challenges now facing the Eurozone are attributable largely to policy errors that can be understood only in terms of "the role of ideas and beliefs": "The founders of the euro were guided by a set of ideas, notions about how economies function, that were fashionable at the time but that were simply wrong. They had faith in markets and lacked an understanding of the limitations of markets and what was required to make them work.... While in most of the world, market fundamentalism has been discredited, especially in the aftermath of the 2008 global financial crisis, those beliefs survive and flourish within the eurozone's dominant power, Germany. They are held with such conviction and certainty, immune to new contrary evidence, that these beliefs are rightly described as an ideology."[26] As an example of Stiglitz's point, one central banker recently described inflation targeting to me as a "fad" of experts at a particular time that was nevertheless picked up on by both international institutions and capital markets as a "necessity" of good governance.

Central bankers are often painfully aware of the limits of their expertise. The fact that neither the movements of financial markets nor the effects of their regulation can be reduced fully to the laws of economics is something any sophisticated expert knows all too well.[27] In his anthropological study of central banks around the world, Douglas Holmes finds that in response to the failures of conventional economic expertise, "central banks cultivate networks of interlocutors that generate knowledge—what amounts to ethnographic knowledge—about the social and cultural character of the economy."[28] This leads him to conclude that "central banking is more of a 'performative art' than a 'predictive science.'"[29]

These doubts have become more widespread and more pronounced of late because markets are no longer behaving as the economic models predict that they should. Many policymakers trained in economics now lament the failure of economics to sufficiently predict or even explain the consequences of current monetary policy or to give us a coherent picture of what is happening in the economy. At a recent Meridian 180 conference, a fascinating discussion broke out among policymakers about how the next financial crisis would be handled. Some argued that a "playbook" for crisis management now exists, thanks to the lessons of the financial crisis of 2008. Others countered that the very nature of a crisis is that there is no playbook—that the expertise garnered from past crises is not sufficient to tell policymakers what to do in the present or how to predict the future.

Mundane Technical Details Are Value-Laden

But central banking is not just about ideas. Day-to-day work within a central bank is defined by routines, procedures, scripts for gathering information, evaluating problems, structuring responses to those problems, and generating consensus for solutions. Central banking is routine technocratic work centered around a series of "techniques" that are used to craft solutions, both large and small, in much the same way that a plumber might repair a leaky valve or an urban planner might craft a new bus route through a growing city.

The work of central banks is not just about high-profile monetary policy. Many other important activities go on inside central banks. This includes crafting regulatory norms, rules, and policies; monitoring banks in order to determine that they are individually and collectively in sound economic condition; acting as "lender of last resort" when a crisis occurs; engaging in formal and informal coordination with other central banks around the world on policy issues; and maintaining the payment system—the system by which payments are cleared between private banks when an individual client of one private bank sends a payment to another.

When central bankers assert that their work is technocratic and not political, they point to these kinds of mundane activities. It is boring stuff—stuff the public could not possibly care about. And yet these things are not just mere technicalities. They have power. I have shown elsewhere how central bankers borrowed many of the tricks and techniques of private market legitimacy to confer legitimacy on central bank practices that otherwise might have been maligned as "political."[30] Let me give an example—the work of designing and maintaining a payment system.

The payment system is the plumbing of the national economy: funds cannot be transferred from one party to another without going through the central bank's back-end clearing infrastructure. The very need for this state-sponsored system is one way in which private markets are always already public.

Central banks have developed elaborate procedures for loaning funds to clearing banks during daytime hours when they may lack sufficient funds to clear their obligations. Without this government-provided liquidity, the market would effectively fail many times per day. There are several different ways of structuring such a clearing mechanism. They all rely on intraday government loans, and hence "cost" the public something and provide a benefit to private banks. Yet the differing details of how payment systems are structured in turn require different routines and procedures within the private banks that use them. Japanese central bankers chose one kind of system, known as real-time gross settlement (RTGS), in part because it encouraged a certain kind of behavior from private actors: it required more individual responsibility, forcing them to think more on their toes and hence to conform more to certain ideals of what good market actors should act like.

In this example, the mundane technicalities of the payment system turn out to have important consequences for how market participants must respond and learn to act. These technicalities actually aim to change what kind of person one must become to act successfully in the market. Indeed, this is one of the purposes of the technicalities, from its architects' point of view. The technical structure of the system becomes a way to mandate certain kinds of behavior and, hopefully, a way to change people's ways of thinking about market activity itself. From this point of view, these mundane technicalities do the very same work governments could do, with laws and regulations, to shape the wider culture of markets.

Obviously, the purpose of the clearing system deployed by the Bank of Japan in this example was not just to change market participants' behavior. It was also to ensure that payments could be resolved efficiently in the Japanese market, and indeed RTGS was the global standard at the time it was adopted in Japan. This is important because we need to appreciate that something can be practical and effective as a good piece of financial engineering and *also* have cultural effects. We do not need to choose between a scientific or a cultural understanding of these technicalities.

Central Bankers and the Public

So expertise is cultural. It is shorthand for speaking to other experts. It is even a style of talking, of dressing, of behaving. At the beginning of this chapter, I described how a Japanese central banker once told me that he feels more at home with other central bankers from around the world than he does with ordinary Japanese people. This common culture of expertise is necessary and desirable, since it allows people to communicate quickly and fluidly about highly complex and technical matters.

Yet a culture of expertise also limits who can be included in the conversation. Most central bankers are quite risk-averse, socially respectable people who take pride in living relatively anonymous lives. They are people who, whatever policy disagreements they have with one another, believe in the system. This is, incidentally, a system in which they have personally succeeded and hence have a stake in. Many therefore have a certain lack of comfort with social activists or people from socially marginal positions or groups who continually point out the problems with that system. Claims that are not couched in particular vocabularies or voiced by persons with certain educational pedigrees run the risk of being dismissed as nonsensical. This set of unspoken cultural preferences influences who is included in the conversation and who is not.

A significant body of social scientific research over the past two decades has demonstrated that expertise confers power and authority.[31] Contrary to the claims experts often make that they are simply cogs in the wheels of larger political processes, or that their actions are deeply constrained by outside facts or processes, this literature shows how experts wield considerable power. When I can credibly assert that I am an expert, others have to listen. For example, encounters between doctors and patients inform how patients think of and even physically experience their own bodies, their lives, and their health.[32] The demarcation of expertise from politics is, moreover, itself a source of power. As Jonathan Kirshner put it at a Meridian 180 conference, "It is a political act to claim you are acting apolitically!" This is not to say that expertise is not necessary or important, or that experts do not know things that nonexperts do not know. But with this power, social science has shown, often comes a lack of critical reflection on the limits of one's own perspective.[33]

Why were the experts unable to foresee the 2008 crisis? Why did they not see the possibility of massive defaults in the housing market leading to wider systemic consequences? Many books, novels, newspaper articles, and even blockbuster films have been devoted to this question. In fact, many people did see the crisis coming, but they were not heard—by virtue of the fact that they did not participate in the intellectual conventions of the time.

There are therefore also costs associated with expert cultures. Experts are not the only clients of the global financial system. Ordinary people are also implicated, both as perpetrators and as victims of risk. The 2008 crisis brought attention to consumers and retail investors as key players and sources of risk in financial markets,[34] and even spawned new regulatory initiatives such as the U.S. Consumer Financial Protection Bureau.[35] We have begun to appreciate the fact that the exclusion of ordinary people's point of view in thinking about the economy has serious consequences for the economy as a whole.

Chapter 4

CULTURE CLASH

Experts and the Public

In the last chapter we saw that central banks are cultural institutions. But what about the relationship between the central bank and the public at large? The response of market and citizenry to central bank communications and policies—and hence the effectiveness and effect of those policies—are also culturally framed. Carlo Tognato, a sociologist of central banks, argues that central banks owe their independence and legitimacy largely to wider cultural elements: "the set of cultural resources and practices that are being mobilized to anchor stability-oriented monetary institutions (i.e., central bank independence and the goal of price/monetary stability) to national identity."[1] He gives the example of the European Central Bank (ECB), which, legally speaking, is the most independent of all central banks, since its independence is enshrined in the Maastricht Treaty and hence cannot be changed by national legislatures. Yet compared with the Bundesbank, Tognato argues, the ECB enjoys far less political latitude in response to a financial crisis. This is because of the place of the Bundesbank and the deutschmark in the wider German psyche and their importance to German postwar political identity.[2] The point is that central bank independence turns on a set of larger cultural assumptions and ideas, and they would be wise to tap into these.

Culture therefore pervades the relationship between central banks and the public and shapes the terms and the limits of the policy options. A good example is the recent struggles of the European Union. The problem with the European project, according to many economists, among them Joseph Stiglitz and Paul Krugman, is that it naïvely presumed that financial integration alone would lead to a more complete integration: "One of the reasons for the failure of the eurozone is that economic integration has outpaced political integration. The hope was that the politics would catch up with the economics. But as divisiveness and the democratic deficit has grown, the likelihood that that will happen has diminished."[3]

Most European policymakers now acknowledge that financial integration is impossible without cultural integration. People need to feel genuinely a part of a common cultural project first. The backlash against European financial integration is, in part, the result of the fact that the euro is as much a unit of cultural accountability as it is a unit of financial accounting. Regardless of the merits of the financial structures, policies, and economic toolkit that undergird it as a currency, one cannot ignore what it stands for, as a matter of a unified European cultural identity. The lesson here for central bankers is clear: if you want to understand your policy options, you must understand the cultural environment in which you operate.

In each country, the political terrain has a slightly different topography. The history and the issues that resonate with the public are different. Differences in corporate culture and differences in consumer spending and saving traditions can mean that the same monetary policy succeeds in one place and fails, or even leads to financial instability, in another. These political, cultural, and social differences can have direct financial implications. For example, former member of the Bank of Japan Policy Committee Sayuri Shirai argued in a recent Meridian 180 forum that Japanese young people's lack of trust in the government is impacting the Japanese financial system, as almost a third refuse to make payments to the national pension system. This would not necessarily be true in the same way elsewhere, both because of the unique institutional configuration of the pension system and because of the particular hopelessness of Japanese youth. This variation needs to be understood as a relevant dimension of financial politics, and incorporated into central bank policymaking because different forms of capitalism produce different kinds of problems and deserve different kinds of responses.[4] So attention to culture clash also demands attention to cultural variations among different countries.

Populism and Finance

All of this leads us to the current political situation in Europe, the United States, and other parts of the world, where we are witnessing muscular demonstrations of populism. One of its targets is the central bank. The government bailouts of domestic and international banks, and the extension of "swap lines" to selected central banks, set the Federal Reserve up as lender of last resort to the world.[5] In the United States, with the Audit the Fed movement on the right and the Occupy Wall Street movement on the left, the central bank has emerged as a target of populist rage. In the United Kingdom, the Bank of England and its governor, Mark Carney, were swept up into the campaign's ambit of discontent with cosmopolitan elites, becoming the target of derogatory statements from crowd-pleasing politicians. There is an increasing lack of public trust in central bankers' ability to avert or manage financial crises. The failure of conventional monetary tools, the use of untested alternatives, and the delayed recovery from the economic crisis have eroded public confidence in central banks' capacity to operate effectively, much less independently.

In a recent survey of twenty advanced European economies across 154 years, Manuel Funke, Moritz Schularick, and Christoph Trebesch found that financial crises correlate significantly with a rise in right-wing populism: "After a crisis, voters seem to be particularly attracted to the political rhetoric of the extreme right, which often attributes blame to minorities or foreigners," the authors write. "On average, far-right parties increase their vote share by 30% after a financial crisis."[6] Financial crises can alter the political and cultural landscape in ways that impact societies on issues far beyond finance.

Yet the roots of popular discontent with central banks are deeper and more diffuse than economics alone. After all, central bankers are not the only targets of popular frustration. The public seems to have lost confidence in experts across the spectrum—from doctors to professors to journalists to climate scientists.

The gulf between experts and the public was long managed by one foundational myth. When anthropologists use the word "myth," we do not mean to suggest that something is false. Rather, a myth is just an idea, an explanation, or a set of assumptions that is fairly universally accepted and provides a justification for given institutional and social relationships. If you do not like the word myth, you can substitute the term "political theory."

The myth was that there are two kinds of things government actors do. Some things are political—those are things that in a democracy are properly decided by the people through their elected officials. Political decisions should be taken by prime ministers, presidents, and legislatures. But there is another category of things that are technical. In this area, the public does not need to be consulted; in fact, the public should not be consulted. Rather, experts should decide what is best for everyone as a whole. The decision to build a bridge may be a political one, but the decision about what materials to use to build it is a technical decision for the engineers. The myth was that there are spheres of life that belong to the public, and there are spheres of life in which it is best to trust the experts.

In the world of central banking, it has long been assumed that most of what central banks do—from monetary policy to bank regulation—is technical, not political, and therefore should be decided by experts. This is the assumption that underlay debates about central bank legitimacy discussed in chapter 2. In the days when the problem was how to control inflation, a number of studies sought to show that central bank independence from politicians correlated with low inflation because, it was argued, politicians made decisions that were popular with constituents in the short run but not in everyone's best interest in the long run. Independent experts, in contrast, were respected because they could make the better but more difficult choices.

Across many domains of culture in many societies, however, this myth of a division of authority grounded in the pure authority of scientific expertise seems to be unraveling. One only has to look at popular culture—movies, science fiction novels, music—to find endless plot lines and verses about experts who do not know how to manage crises, or who are acting for their own benefit rather than the benefit of the public at large. In the wider society, we witness an increasingly politicized encounter of expert versus nonexpert cultures. The public has increasingly lost confidence in expertise itself.

The sources of this cultural shift are multiple and complex. The Hollywood story line of the incompetent, corrupt, or dangerous expert builds upon a strand of academic thought that has been prevalent in the academy since the 1970s. Loosely labeled postmodernism or poststructuralism, this strand of thought challenges the authority of experts and the authoritative status of science. Media studies experts have also noted the impact of changes in media structures over the past ten years, from a "hierarchically organized system" in which "news and other information flowed downstream from centralized news organizations to audiences," to an Internet-based system in which "audiences have more input into the news system and more control over the flow of news."[7]

Yet to all these wider sources of populist anger against central banks we should add the actions of central banks themselves. Federal Reserve funds were used in the last crisis to bail out financial firms outside the United States. Banks and bankers in London, Frankfurt, and Tokyo were saved by loans from U.S. taxpayers. The fact that these loans were ultimately paid back with interest and that there were good economic reasons for the Federal Reserve's actions does not change the fact that these policies, and the failure fully to engage the public in their crafting and implementation, had other *cultural* effects.

Anthropologists have studied what has happened in many societies when core myths are destroyed, either through colonialism, invasion, modernization, or conversion. For example, the Japanese people at one point claimed to believe that their emperor was a god. One key goal of U.S. general Douglas MacArthur's occupation project was to demonstrate to the Japanese people that the emperor was just an ordinary man. He attempted to do this by summoning the emperor to General Headquarters and staging a now iconic photograph of this tiny man standing next to the towering MacArthur. In such cases, there will always be a radical few who try to return to the old faith—in Japan, they show up on the emperor's birthday waving flags and shouting slogans—but even for them, things are not like before. That faith now has to be continually defended. For the majority, it is impossible to go back.

So today, the central bank is on the public's radar. Populist attacks are framed explicitly as attacks on the expertise of central bankers. The trigger for these attacks is the fact that the economic impact of central bank interventions is less and less predictable. In defiance of mainstream economic theory, major central bank stimulus measures often produce little response from the market. This has fueled public doubts about the expertise of central bankers and indeed the need for independent central banks. The following blog post from the Breitbart website is representative of the new right-wing populist rhetoric. It moves from a mocking distrust of experts' claims to authority to threats of possible violence:

> The Federal Reserve is often spoken about as if it possesses some divine intelligence. Reminiscent of the EF Hutton commercials, the CNBC crowd behaves similarly, falling all over themselves to dissect every word for some hidden message or insight—when, in fact, there isn't one. Most of the Fed's statements can be best surmised by Shakespeare:
>
> > It is a tale. Told by an idiot, full of sound and fury,
> > Signifying nothing.
>
> > —Macbeth Act 5, scene 5
>
> The Fed is essentially a one-trick pony that attempts to solve every problem by juicing the system. Sold to the public as above the fold, and a group beyond reproach, they and their fellow Central bank accomplices around the world are creating a massive sovereign debt crisis that can never be unwound with sound money or honest accounting.
>
> . . .
>
> The rise in popularity of Bernie Sanders and Donald Trump is a clear sign that the public is waking up to the high-stakes games being played in the financial arena, and what losing ultimately costs them. There will be an ocean of tears to be shed by the masses if these problems are not addressed and dealt with appropriately. . . . The real fear, however, is that the next time something seriously goes wrong, what if the people of these United States pick up pitch forks in lieu of ballots?[8]

What all this suggests is that the story experts tell about central banks as technocratic machines, and about central bankers as financial engineers without values of their own, no longer convinces the public at large, the politicians, or insiders themselves. It has ceased to serve any useful cultural purpose. It also suggests that the cultural effects of central bank policies are critically important. They matter independently of the economic effects of central bank policies.

Nationalism and Globalism

In many cases, this anti-expert populism fuses with new forms of nationalism. Abe and Trump both came to power as nationalists who promised to force the central bank to yield to their agendas for the good of the nation. In the United States, attacks on the Federal Reserve were launched at the same political rallies and from the same political mouthpieces as calls of "America First" and "Make America Great Again." Likewise, in the UK, pro-Brexit politicians decried the European Central Bank as a bunch of faceless "Bureaucrats in Brussels" acting without supervision and against British national interests.

It is an interesting irony that central banks should emerge as targets of nationalism. Historically, central banks have often been the economic engines of nationalist projects. Most of the great wars have been financed by central bank monetary policies, and, indeed, in Japan today one powerful argument for central bank independence, in an era of rising nationalism, is that it is important not to repeat the past.

Yet in many parts of the world, we have seen popular misgivings about globalization of late. People are crying foul on some of the promises made on behalf of globalization over the past several decades—promises that without borders, all will be better off financially. They point out that even if, on average, everyone benefits from globalization, there are distributional effects. Some benefit a great deal, while others (for example, workers whose jobs are relocated) suffer more than their fair share. The globalization dream did not adequately address the inequalities globalization inevitably creates on the way to creating a bigger pie for all.

Likewise, the promise of globalization was that economic integration would inevitably lead to cultural integration. The experience of the European Union has amply demonstrated that this is not the case: economic integration without adequate attention to cultural and political differences is a recipe for political as well as economic disaster.

How central banks respond to nationalist pressure, in turn, shapes the wider political and cultural environment. In the European case, central banks have been involved in efforts to craft a more cosmopolitan political narrative to counter rising nationalism. Anthropologist Doug Holmes argues that we should understand many of ECB president Mario Draghi's speeches, and indeed the policies of the ECB more generally, as attempts to create a political conversation that will build the groundwork for a palatable pan-European political identity. Likewise, in Sweden, Holmes argues, central bankers are using talk about the market to engage in a political project of nation and region building (Holmes 2014).

It would be far too simplistic to suggest that central bank policies and pronouncements are either causes of, or bulwarks against, populist nationalism. Yet there is no doubt that central banks are now drawn into an unfolding nationalist cultural moment. Central bank policies participate in the emergence of new cultural narratives. Their actions may contribute to the crystallization of new group identities. We could even say that they may give rise to new moods, new cultural moments. What we normally think of only in terms of financial or economic policy turned out to be profoundly culturally transformative. In the next chapter we will begin to think about what to do about this.

Chapter 5

Toward Financial Citizenship and a New Legitimacy Narrative

In the last chapter we faced the problem: a cultural divide between experts and ordinary people has festered into a political conflict that threatens to become a political crisis. So what can we do about it? That is the question for the remainder of this book.

All of us—experts and publics alike—need to address this legitimacy crisis head on, for the sake of the health of both our economies and our democracies. And so the first thing that we need, if we are to turn this situation around, is a different vision of where we might be headed collectively.

This new vision has two important parts. The first part I will call *financial citizenship*—it is a vision of a new role for citizens in the stewardship and governance of the economy and a new partnership between experts and publics. The second part I will call a new *legitimacy narrative* for central banks: we need to agree together on a new explanation for why the work of central banks is important—something better than a statement from central bankers to the effect of "just trust us—we're the experts and we know best." This new shared understanding can emerge only from a dialogue across our cultural differences, that is, from living out a new ideal of financial citizenship.

All this will not be easy. I know that many central bankers will react with skepticism about the possibility of engaging the public and even with outright hostility to the idea that we must open up and break down the boundaries between cultures. But if we do this, I believe, we can put our financial governance institutions back on legitimate political ground.

From Investor Education to Financial Citizenship

Central bankers think about how and why to engage with the broader public relatively rarely. But when they do, they usually think in terms of "investor education." Many central banks have museums aimed at tourists and schoolchildren, for example. If you visit these museums you will see old coins, or portraits of founding fathers of the central bank, or perhaps a few bars of gold. Exhibitions and materials explaining the basics of the financial markets and how to save and invest are all part of most central banks' investor education activities.

Investor education is clearly important for helping individual consumers to make good financial decisions. Yet investor education has a critical flaw: the purpose of this learning is simply to improve ordinary people's personal financial decisions—to produce more informed and more rational participants in the financial markets. It is not to engage the public in a serious dialogue about the central bank's political mandate.

Most recently, some central banks have made a very limited effort to go beyond investor education, with museum tours and speeches that explain more fully what central banks do and why it is important. Although the limited staff time devoted to such projects reflects the lack of appreciation in many central banks on how crucial this work is, this is of course a most important development. It needs to be radically expanded through dramatic increases in staffing and creative partnerships with educators at the K–12 and higher education levels, with NGOs, with employers, with local political authorities.

Yet as well intended as these introductions to central bank work may be, they still have a critical limitation. They assume that education is unidirectional—that the central bank experts will do the teaching about what goes on in central banks, for the benefit of the ordinary public's learning. These are not forums for discussion but forums for pedagogy.

If the central banks imagine no real forum for ordinary people to debate and engage them about their proper roles, other institutions have stepped in to fill the gap. In the United States, for example, online discussion boards and comment sections of fringe media on both the right and the left are filled with ordinary people expressing their views about the proper functions of the central bank. These spaces are rife with false information, and in cases may even become incubators of conspiracy theories.[1] In these spaces, people unfortunately usually only encounter other people who already share their views, and often score points and capture attention by framing those views in terms of outrageous slogans and sound bites.

This balkanization of the public sphere is of course counterproductive and even dangerous. But it does demonstrate one important point: many people are interested in what central banks do, and willing to devote time to engaging in a dialogue of sorts about it. The question therefore is how to bring those people into a more constructive and transformative dialogue for all sides.

What Financial Citizenship Means

I want to propose a different goal. Rather than investor education, we need a new era of financial citizenship. By financial citizenship I mean the act of taking responsibility for the normative choices inherent in financial governance. In other words, I mean a role far beyond voting with one's pocketbook or taking responsibility for one's financial decisions.[2] The economist Charles Goodhart has argued that choosing the appropriate balance between competing priorities is "an essential part of the democratic process, and should not be delegated."[3] Yet if the public should not delegate this important task, then it stands to reason that the public needs to take responsibility for making these choices. The alternative is a power vacuum in which powerful interest groups—especially the financial industry—become the only voice and come to dictate the policy choices of legislators.

Citizenship of course requires education too. From our youth, we learn a great deal about our government, our heritage, and the world beyond so that we can exercise our citizenship rights wisely and effectively. One cannot be an effective citizen without a working understanding of the issues. In other spheres in which each of us exercises our citizenship rights, moreover, we understand well that education does not stop with the end of a person's formal education in their youth. Public libraries, independent media, and journalistic ethics are all critical to our democracies because they give citizens an opportunity to educate themselves. These same institutions have a critical role to play in a new financial citizenship. I will say more about that in the next chapter.

In much the same way as in other areas of citizenship, financial citizenship requires the public to have a working understanding of how the national and global financial system operates, and about the important role state institutions such as central banks play in the stability of the financial markets and why this stability is crucial to the ordinary person's livelihood. It also requires knowledge of more than the textbook nuts and bolts: people need some form of understanding of the lives and work of the experts, as intelligent, highly trained, and specialized professionals who for the most part are extremely dedicated to public service, and who work long hours on difficult tasks. This picture of what *central bankers* do, not just what *central banks* do, must also include a more unvarnished and subtle (and hence believable) picture of experts as people with limitations—people who by nature of their specialization do not always understand everything about the economy as it is experienced by people on the street, who may not even be fully aware of the biases that come with their membership in an expert culture. This complex view of the experts is the necessary starting point for a better collaborative relationship with the public.

Yet citizenship is not *just* about information. It is also about commitment. As citizens, all of us understand that making responsible and ethical choices about the future of our government is a responsibility as well as a privilege that defines the strength of our democracies. We understand that our democratic institutions are a commons, like a public park, whose present-day quality and future security turn on whether we each act individually to protect the common good. Citizenship is about duties, not just rights.

In the same way, financial citizenship is about commitment to participation—to doing what each of us can to further the strength of our collective national and international economic well-being.

In an earlier book, I have written about how each of us plays a critical role in the governance of the market in ways we may not understand.[4] For example, when a lawyer drafts a contract between two parties well and ensures that the parties are well informed about their bargain, she helps to bring stability to one small corner of the market. The U.S. experience with the subprime mortgage crisis taught us how important this kind of ordinary market governance can be by showing us what can happen when it is not there. Likewise, when ordinary consumers read and reflect on the small print in the contracts they sign, or take the time to complain to authorities about small incidents of fraud that can affect others, they are contributing to market stability.

But each of us also has a role to play in financial governance by engaging constructively with the experts and the policymakers. For example, how should the difficult trade-offs between the negative distributive consequences of interest rate policy and the positive benefits of financial stability be handled? There is no right answer to this question. It is a normative question, a question of value judgments. What to do about the trade-off depends on your vision of what the individual and common good looks like. We cannot just leave this question to experts and then complain when their choices do not conform to our desires. Even worse, we cannot pretend that there are no value judgments at stake in this question, and then accuse the experts of being ineffective or even corrupt for failing to make the value choice we might have wanted them to make.

Of course, being a good citizen does not mean agreeing with everything that one's leaders do. On the contrary, there is a long and distinguished tradition of loyal political dissent in the name of citizenship. In much the same way, financial citizenship does not mean that one cannot criticize the central bank. It is not a tool of the central bank for ensuring popular buy-in for its policies. Yet there is a difference between critique and conspiracy theories, between a reasoned and principled criticism or a call for change, and an effort to score political points with one's political base at the expense of experts. Sometimes the difference may be subtle, and the line between the two may be open to different interpretations, but there is a difference nonetheless. The point is that there must be a role for citizens in the governance of the economy.

Financial citizenship is a cause that demands a commitment from each of us. All of us have a stake in financial citizenship because the things we all value most, from the security of our retirements to the stability of our democratic process, depend on it. Think of financial citizenship as what Duvvuri

Subbarao, former governor of the Reserve Bank of India, has termed a "global public good"[5]—something valuable that belongs to us all, just like our democratic process. The paradox of public goods is that we all enjoy them only to the extent that each of us is generous enough to maintain them. We understand how this is true of the democratic process: the vibrancy of our political institutions depends on each of us making the time and effort to participate, with care, in local, national, and global institutions. It depends on engaging others through the political process with honesty and empathy, and in acting with integrity for the greater good of all. The same is true of financial citizenship: it shapes all of our individual welfares, and our individual well-being depends on our collective investment in the quality of the process. We have a citizenship duty to maintain and to strengthen our economic governance as we address the challenges to come. We need national—and indeed, given the global character of financial markets—global conversations about the rights and duties of citizens and of government officials and financial institutions. I will say more about how we can concretely begin to do this in the next chapter. But first, let us turn to the second prong of our vision for change, a new legitimacy narrative for central banking.

A New Legitimacy Narrative

As important as financial citizenship is, it is not enough. We also need a new agreement about why central banks exist, what they do, why it matters, and what the rights and obligations of respective political and economic actors are vis-à-vis central banks. Let's call this new agreement a new legitimacy narrative for central banking.

As we have seen in the previous chapters, the old explanation or story about why central banks exist and why unelected experts within central banks have the authority that they do is no longer entirely convincing. It needs updating in light of political, cultural, and economic changes.

This new legitimacy narrative is critical because it will provide the foundation for collective action, as well as further conversation about choices and trade-offs, in moments of crisis. It is critical because it will give central bankers' work value and provide a pathway for thinking through day-to-day policy choices in ordinary times. It is critical because in the absence of a reasoned and principled legitimacy narrative, demagogues on all sides will fill the gap with self-serving and ultimately destructive narratives of their own.

This new shared understanding cannot be just government PR. It can only come from dialogue across the cultural differences we have been exploring in this book. The result must be something that seems authentic, and accurate, and actionable to all the relevant parties—bureaucrats, financiers, members of the public.

Therefore the new legitimacy narrative can only be the outcome of a process—a formal conversation. In the next chapter I will provide some suggestions as to how such a conversation could be staged. But what is crucial here is that neither side—neither the public nor the experts—holds all the pieces of the puzzle. We will have to put them together in a way that makes sense for both. And the pieces of that puzzle, as well as its ultimate contours, shades, and themes, will no doubt differ from one nation to the next: the story that fits best in Tokyo most likely will not be identical to the story that fits best in Canberra or Washington or Brussels.

However, if central bankers, members of the media, the academy, the NGO community, and the public at large embrace the challenge creatively and forcefully, we can set a new course. One European experience is instructive: In Denmark, successive central bank governors have understood the necessity of holding a dialogue with the public about the importance of the central bank in terms that resonate with the wider cultural orientation of the Danish people. Anders Sørensen describes how generations of Danish central bank governors have skillfully drawn upon themes in Danish national identity to engage the broader public in a discussion of the central bank's policies and its political authority to act. He argues that they have succeeded because they had the right "narrative"—"a symbolic representation of events that is framed by a certain theme and linked in time."[6] For many Danes, the notion of consensus is a core feature of their national identity. It is what defines the polity. For this reason, central bankers have framed their policies in terms of appeals to social consensus and social solidarity. The result, Sørensen argues, is not simply that the central bank has gained political support for its policies, but that a healthy and independent central bank became "embedded in national identity." As a result, support for the central bank became a part of the citizenry's support for the nation. This enviable position was possible, Sørensen adds, only because the central bank's governors understood that "the language of science" was "insufficient to promote their monetary policies."[7]

Although there will be variation from country to country in this narrative, and although we cannot dictate at the outset exactly what it will be, we are nevertheless not completely in the dark about the direction in which we will go. We can already see the contours of what the new legitimacy narrative will be. So here are some key elements that we will want to include in a new understanding of why central banks are necessary and when their actions are legitimate.

KEY ELEMENT #1: RESILIENCE

Central banks are legitimate when they help build resilient economies and resilient nations.[8] Resilience is a value we all share; it is about surviving and thriving in the face of cultural, political, and economic change. All of us have an interest in the resilience of our nation and of our national economy.

KEY ELEMENT #2: INTERDEPENDENCE

Resilience in turn is a relationship. It requires a partnership between all participants in the economy, across national and international political, cultural, and economic differences. And hence a second key element is recognition of our interdependence. For example, we cannot speak of national economic resilience without considering the health of the global economy in a world in which national economies are so interdependent. Likewise, thinking about the resilience of our national economy requires us to understand the interdependence of different sectors of the economy, and hence why risky behavior in one sector impacts all the rest, or why sometimes it may be necessary to bail out one sector, or provide government subsidies to another, for the benefit of the whole.

In particular, markets and states are independent. One of the reasons it is hard to see central banking for what it is has to do with our assumptions about the relationship between the market and the state. In the common understanding, states are political entities (governments), but markets are not political. This understanding is the legacy of neoliberalism, a philosophy that achieved remarkable global authority from the 1980s until, roughly, the

2008 financial crisis. In this understanding, states are suspect things. The best kind of political system is a system in which the state is ostensibly small and weak, while as much authority as possible devolves to the market. According to this theory, states and markets are quite distinct forms of social organization.

The claim that (good) markets were and should be something quite distinct from (bad) states always posed a special challenge for central banks: If markets are entirely self-sustaining, why should we need central banks—state banks—in the first place? Can't the market correct itself without the need for the government to inject cash at certain times or restrict liquidity at other times? Can't the markets police themselves without government monitoring and regulations? Indeed, one of the great fathers of neoliberalism, Friedrich Hayek, made just this claim—that central banks were a blight on capitalism and should be eliminated. In my own ethnographic research among central bankers I found a considerable amount of personal angst among them about this contradiction: central bankers are people who believe strongly in capitalism. So, if capitalism works so well, what justification is there for their own role?

Yet the fact is that markets and states are not independent—they are interdependent. In her history of money, Christine Desan has shown how this idea that central banks—and by extension states—are separate from markets is not just false now, but has been false since the very beginning of modern money.[9] Desan shows how the production of money was, from its inception, a sovereign political project, not a private market affair simply bolstered or bounded by state law. She shows how the central bank was, at its inception, a hybrid of public and private interests, and how it has remained a kind of hinge between the state and the market, or rather a place where it becomes apparent that the two cannot be separated. Hayek's fantasy of a world without central banks notwithstanding, most modern economists understand that financial markets are simply unsustainable without constant state intervention and regulation. For their part, nation-states are entirely reliant on private financial markets to finance all their public sovereign activities through government debt—as they have been, Desan shows, from the very start. It seems we are stuck with a messy world in which public and private are mixed up and interdependent.

Once we accept that central banks are both private and public, both state institutions and market institutions, and that markets and states are inseparable conceptually and functionally, we can understand that markets and states both need central banks, just as each needs the other. In a market already mixed up with the sovereign's interests, the central bank is a kind of hinge, a flash point of interconnection between public and private.

Focusing on interdependence requires a change in mind-set. As we saw in chapter 2, the old legitimacy narrative focused not on interdependence, but on independence. Legitimacy turned on explaining why experts should be independent of the political process, and the legitimacy of central banks was often defined in terms of how independent from the political process they actually were. In contrast, the new legitimacy narrative will explore all of the ways that good central banking is interdependent with the actions of others in society, politics, and markets.

KEY ELEMENT #3: COLLABORATION AND TRUST

The third key element flows from the second. If central banks cannot act alone, if one sector of the economy is interdependent with the next, if your political and economic interests are intertwined with mine, then there is no way forward except through collaboration. We need to define in broad terms and also in very concrete ones what kind of collaboration is necessary to govern the economy, and what kind of collaboration is necessary among different sectors of the economy.

For a long time, we thought we did not have to think about collaboration and trust in a market economy. The institution of price was supposed to take care of all of that. But the failures of many markets to price assets correctly have already led to a focus on collaboration as an alternative to, or enhancement of, price in many sectors of the economy. The so-called collaborative economy is already a force in most people's lives. It remains for us to better understand how and why collaboration can also play a central role in the governance of the economy.

This is a more radical change to the old legitimacy narrative than meets the eye. Where the old narrative focused on carving out separate spheres of autonomy for citizens and experts, the new legitimacy narrative will focus on collaboration between these groups. As we saw in earlier chapters, the old reigning myth posited a distinction between technical and political issues, with the former delegated to experts and the latter delegated to the public through its elected officials. But a focus on collaboration allows us to imagine the world very differently. Rather than a clear divide between technical and political issues, we now see the universe of market governance as a continuum between highly technical questions and highly political ones, with most issues involving some mix of both. This means that in most cases, in order for central bank actions to be legitimate, both experts and the public must be involved, because both have critical contributions to make. Each side must be open to the legitimate "interference" of the other in its decision making, for the benefit of all.

Obviously, collaboration is impossible without trust. There is already a great deal of economic and sociological literature on the significance of trust for markets. Many economists think of trust as a kind of public good—something that benefits us all. However, we need a much more concrete and detailed conversation about how to build trust among different sectors in the economy, and across political divides. We need a better understanding of how the public and the experts can come to trust one another, and how this trust can be built and maintained, as well as what the risks or impediments to trust might be.

As we have seen throughout this book, expertise alone no longer guarantees public trust. Another possible rationale for legitimacy is delegated political authority: the legislature, as the legitimate representative of the people, has delegated certain powers to the central bank, it can be said, and the exercise of those powers is therefore legitimate. Yet as we saw, in practice, delegated authority is also an incomplete foundation for public trust—because the public holds its elected officials in as much disregard as the experts, because that authority can always be revoked, and because delegation of authority does not resolve questions in the public mind about the motivations and social networks of the experts.

So why should the public trust the experts? Of course, expertise remains an important part of the answer. Of course, central banks must have properly delegated authority to act. Yet in addition to this, central bankers need to be able to say to the public: "Trust us also because we listen carefully and engage with you seriously. Trust us because we have internal mechanisms for processing what we learn from this engagement into policy. Trust us because we have mechanisms for reflecting critically on how well we engage the public. Trust us because we have mechanisms for reflecting critically on our own culturally determined blind spots."

And why should the experts trust the public? We rarely asked this question because we assume a model of public service in which the public servant has no legitimate right to admit distrust in the public. But the fact is that without mutual trust there can be no collaboration, so we need to ask this question. How can the public gain the trust of the experts? In fact, the answer must be much the same. The community of NGOs, the media, and other organizations interested in financial governance need to demonstrate their commitment to financial citizenship in the way we have described it in the previous pages. They need to be able to say: "Trust us because we listen carefully. Trust us because when we criticize, it is a place of shared commitments to the resilience of our economy. Trust us because even when we disagree about policy directions, we respect your expertise, your judgment, and your commitment to your task."

KEY ELEMENT #4: HARD CHOICES

Financial governance involves hard choices. Any policy entails trade-offs. Some people will benefit more than others. Some may actually be harmed. Often such hard choices take place in a context of significant unknowns. Too often, the conversation between the public and the experts has not acknowledged this simple fact. And yet the very reason the legitimacy of central banking turns on a collaborative relationship with the public is precisely the fact of hard choices.

We need to have a much more serious and detailed conversation about the hard choices involved in financial governance. Only with this conversation can the public voice views on those choices and trade-offs. At the same time, the public needs to understand that experts have no easy solutions, and they need to share with the experts the responsibility for intended and unintended outcomes of those hard choices.

KEY ELEMENT #5: CULTURE CLASH

Finally, a new legitimacy narrative must entail some recognition of the cultural problem we have been discussing throughout this book. That is, both sides—the experts and publics—need to recognize that their own view is the product of the culture that surrounds them. They also need to recognize that the views of others are a product of their own culture as well. In other words, all of us have blind spots, and all of us have tastes in everything from who we spend time with to what ideas appeal to us. This does not mean that we cannot hold particular normative or scientific commitments. But it does mean that we should be open to considering, and maybe even exploring, their limitations by engaging with people outside our own cultural milieu.

Chapter 6

A Program for Action

The core message of this book is that finding a way to manage the culture clash that permeates policy around central banking is vitally important. It affects us deeply and directly and hence is worthy of the investment of our civic energy. So how can we do this, concretely? What steps can each of us take? What institutional reforms might help us to take those steps? This is the subject of this chapter.

Meet the Critics Half Way

First, it is time for central bankers to meet their populist critics half way and to acknowledge, as Janet Yellen failed to do when faced with candidate Trump's attacks, that central banking *is* political in the following specific sense: central bankers are cultural actors, and there are value choices at stake in the technical work of central banking. This is *not* to say that central bankers are politically *partisan* (favoring one political party or one political candidate over another). Nor is it to say that they always or intentionally act in a way that favors one social, political, or economic group at the expense of another. Central bankers rightly bristle at that kind of simplistic attack. But lacking a better explanation for their actions, they retreat behind an equally caricatured public persona of the technocratic machine.

What we need instead is a richer understanding of culture and value choices—as something ubiquitous, unavoidable, legitimate, important, highly complex, and entirely compatible with scientific and financial expertise. While expertise is real and necessary, it entails not just technical choices but ethical and political choices. Indeed, central bankers need to embrace and learn to communicate with the public about this more sophisticated understanding of the politics of expertise. Only then will they be able to honestly and clearly explain why they are *not* motivated by narrow partisan politics, as some critics suggest.

Any dialogue between policymakers and the public therefore needs to begin from the standpoint of recognizing the empirical reality of value judgments. Yet when faced with this reality, most financial analysts will begin to feel entirely out of the zone of their expertise. Were the social transformations brought about by Abenomics on the whole positive or negative? How would one begin to answer such a question? Isn't this a question for political scientists, philosophers, or anthropologists rather than for economists?

Yes, it is a question for political scientists, philosophers, and anthropologists—but it is also a question for the public at large. We need to begin to use normative words, alongside economic terms, to discuss financial policy choices. In an environment in which robust political consequences of central bank policies overshadow relatively weak economic effects of those policies, values, choices, and our conflicting visions of the good life need to become a central focus in public conversations about central banking.

Acknowledge the Distributive Consequences of Central Bank Activities

In particular, central bankers need to publicly acknowledge and give more policy attention to the fact that, as discussed in chapter 2, there are significant distributive consequences to central bank actions. During the 2016 U.S. presidential campaign, Judy Shelton, a member of the Trump economic advisory council responded in the *Financial Times* to Janet Yellen's statement that politics play no role in central banks' activities by highlighting the distributive effects of Fed policies. Was the Fed partisan? "Not explicitly, perhaps," she acknowledged. "But the central bank can hardly be exempted from the ramifications of its powerful role in distributing economic rewards. The Fed has adopted *monetary policy decisions* that channel low-cost funding to wealthy investors and corporate borrowers at the expense of people with ordinary bank savings accounts and retirees on fixed-income pensions. That is not only inherently political—it is antithetical to the American principle of treating all citizens equally."[1]

On the whole, banks and the bankers have benefited tremendously from the Federal Reserve's loose monetary policies since the financial crisis of 2008. Ordinary investors and workers who are not as invested in the stock markets, however, have not shared in the windfall to the same degree. For those who do not have sufficient cash or expertise to invest in the stock market, savings stagnates in accounts that earn almost no interest at all. Likewise, growth in wages has not mirrored increases in corporate profits.

Contrary to what some populist commentators might suggest, the reason officials inside treasury departments and central banks support loose monetary policies and bailouts in times of crisis is not that they wish to rob small business and working people or a gift to financial elites. The reason they choose these policies is that they believe that doing nothing at a time of crisis would be even worse for ordinary people. Many economic historians believe that the Great Depression of 1929, with all of the misery it brought with it, could have been avoided if the U.S. government had pursued a looser monetary policy. Many economists argue that if the Bush administration had not allowed Lehman Brothers to fail in 2008, the effects of the recession on ordinary people would have been much less severe.

Nevertheless, as Judy Shelton correctly suggested, the decisions of technocrats have profound distributive consequences. And these consequences raise questions about the inherent justice of technocratic rule. As economist Joseph Stiglitz explains: "Monetary policy, as technical as it may seem, has long been recognized as being political: inflation reduces the real value of what debtors owe, helping them at the expense of creditors. No wonder, then, that bankers and bond market investors rail so strongly against inflation. On the other hand, the fight against inflation typically entails raising interest rates, which lowers growth and hurts employment and workers.

Balancing inflation and unemployment is, or should be, a political decision."[2]

Central banks' new "qualitative easing" or "extraordinary monetary policy" tools that extend beyond purchases of government debt to purchases of stock and other specific assets make the matter a whole lot worse. When the central bank, with its enormous resources, purchases a particular asset, it drives the price of that asset up relative to other assets. This benefits those who already own it and can therefore sell for more than before. Purchases that benefit some in society more than others entail "picking winners and losers" among market participants and the citizenry.

Regulatory and financial cooperation among central banks around the world has international distributive consequences as well as national ones. The political economy of global financial inequality, framed by complicated economic and political legacies of colonialism, continues to undergird policymaking at international fora. Certain powerful and wealthy countries' central banks, with histories of cooperation that stretch back a hundred years or more,[3] prop up one another's economies by sharing resources— they agree to support one another by extending credit to one another (so-called swap lines) in times of crisis. These powerful countries (primarily in the North Atlantic) also control the global financial policy agenda, while other, weaker countries have less of a say. Although the principal post-crisis financial regulatory body, the Financial Stability Board (FSB) is a secretariat-like arm of the G20, in practice, the G8 nations (France, Germany, Italy, United Kingdom, Japan, United States, and Russia) have the overwhelming power in setting the agenda. As a result, the post-2008 reforms to the global financial order have targeted issues of primary concern to developed economies with advanced financial markets. As legal scholar Katharina Pistor puts it: "Countries at the top of the global hierarchy owe their position to historical contingencies, for example as winners of world wars (the US) or beneficiaries of cold wars (Germany). Their position has been enhanced by the fact that they (the G10) controlled the rules of the game for global finance set forth in the Basel Concordat and the Basel Accords, and not coincidentally, by the prowess of the financial centers they house. . . . Those at the apex of the system tend to exercise discretionary powers in times of crisis over whether to intervene and whom to rescue."[4]

So central bank policies have distributive effects. As Adam Posen suggested long ago, "there's no institutional fix for politics"—the redistributive struggle over monetary policy is endemic to what central banks do.[5] This is a simple fact, and it is also an obvious fact: ordinary citizens can see it and understand it. As Stiglitz points out, it was quite obvious to ordinary Greek citizens that the European Central Bank's decision not to bail out Greek banks had the effect of forcing citizens to accept extraordinary sacrifices demanded by private investors.

Yet the dominant paradigm for understanding the actions of central banks has paid remarkably little attention to these larger distributive consequences of central bank policies. Some political scientists and nonorthodox economists have stressed this point for years. And since the crisis of 2008, a growing number of commentators acknowledge that the distributional consequences of central bank policies are real. Yet prevalent frameworks for evaluating central bank policies do not place these distributional concerns squarely at the center of the discussion.

Ordinary people are understandably frustrated with expert talk that seems to miss the elephant in the room—the fact that what central banks do can exacerbate income inequalities in society. *So a first step central bankers can take would be to acknowledge far more actively that, just like any other form of public policy, their work has unavoidable distributional effects.*

One reason central bankers feel uncomfortable about these distributive effects is that under the dominant approach to central bank legitimacy, disparate distributive effects of a government agency's policies might be reason for deference to the legislature. Former Bank of England vice governor Paul Tucker, for example, argues that where there are disparate effects any agency (including the central bank) should leave policymaking to elected officials.[6] Yet the problem with this purist view of central bank policymaking in a world in which elected officials lack the competence or the organizational set-up to make day-to-day financial policy decisions is that it creates a catch-22: either one publicly denies distributive effects and opens oneself up for legitimate critique from the public for duplicity, or one recognizes the reality of distributive effects and opens oneself up for legitimate critique for exceeding the boundaries of legitimate authority of nonelected officials.

The fact is that almost all policymaking (not just central banking) has distributive effects. And the fact is that elected officials simply cannot take charge of all areas of government. And so we need a different understanding of where legitimacy might come from in cases in which policymaking is handled by unelected officials and yet there are distributive consequences to those policies. Ironically, however, achieving a more sustainable form of legitimacy for central banking in such "impure" conditions turns on central bankers' willingness to acknowledge a chink in their armor—that what central banks do has distributive consequences.

Acknowledge the Political Consequences of Central Bank Activities

Likewise, central bankers need to acknowledge that central banking has not just economic consequences but political consequences. As we have seen throughout this book, central bank policies have important political effects beyond their economic effects. Yet there is no place to acknowledge these effects in the economic models, no way to take them into consideration when making policy. Of course, the most skilled central bankers are keenly interested in such effects, but they do not, for the most part, write or talk about such things publicly. Nor do their tools help to design policies that take into account such political consequences. Yet if central banks' actions have political effects, then we must begin to think about the central bank and the public as interdependent too. The actions of the central bank may contribute to changes in the public mood and the emergence of particular political coalitions.

For example, there is an argument to be made that in the United States, the bank bailouts of 2008 and the public anger these generated were one of the factors that set the stage politically for the populist movement that produced President Trump. Likewise, in Japan, although many commentators believe that Abenomics has failed as an economic program, it arguably has succeeded as a political program: without Abenomics we might not have Abe. And even more importantly, it has succeeded as a cultural program: Abenomics gave Japanese people something to hope for; it changed the national mood even if its economic promises turned out to be false. Historians likewise have argued that central bank policies during the interwar period directly and indirectly contributed to the rise of fascism and the Second World War.[7] To the extent that such dramatic and far-reaching political consequences of central bank economic policies are foreseeable, policymakers should take these into account in formulating economic policy.

So a second important step central bankers can take is to acknowledge that, as we saw in chapter 2, central banks are in practice not independent but interdependent institutions. Central bankers must acknowledge that their actions intimately depend on, as well as impact, the actions of politicians, of other branches of government, of market participants, and of the public at large.

Bridge the Cultural Chasm

The third thing central bankers need to do is to address the clash of cultures between experts and publics head on. Above all else, they must find a way to bridge the cultural chasm that now separates central bankers (along with other financial regulators, their academic interlocutors, and sophisticated market participants) from the general public. How does this small village open up a bit more to the outside world?

Policymakers need to put a far greater priority on this engagement with the citizenry. Insufficient attention has been paid to the perspectives of consumers, citizens, and civil society groups—How do they interpret or misinterpret central bank actions and communications? What does the economy look like from the points of view of various sectors of society? On one point, at least, citizens' groups have a quite legitimate complaint about the financial governance "elites": financial regulators are woefully out of touch with the thinking and experience of ordinary people within their own nation-states and beyond. This is no longer acceptable for reasons both economic and political.

For example, Abenomics was about one thing—changing ordinary consumers' confidence about the future of the economy and encouraging the consumer to spend money rather than hoarding it. The way this ordinary consumer was understood and talked about, however, remains absurdly out of touch with the real lives of those consumers. Policymakers and financial reporters refer to how the so-called Mrs. Watanabes—hypothetical retail investors—would respond to central bank initiatives. This is a reference to the fact that in Japan housewives are the holders of the family purse strings. But this abstract Mrs. Watanabe belies the fact that in Japan, financial policymakers and bankers are overwhelmingly male, and for the most part leave participation in the ordinary household economy to their wives.

Bankers and policymakers had precious little information about what real investors and consumers would do. If you wanted to know what Mrs. Watanabe would do, you had only to ask some of the millions of real Mrs. Watanabes out there. Yet the real Mrs. Watanabes were almost never consulted by the largely male bureaucrats within the central bank, despite the fact that many of them were surely their spouses, mothers, sisters, and daughters.

The speeches of Governor Kuroda, with catchy slogans, about how the central bank would act to increase interest rates in the future, were aimed to appeal to the so-called Mrs. Watanabes. Kuroda's assumption was that these consumers would be convinced by simple messaging and buzzwords. Yet in the aftermath of Abenomics' failure to change consumers' behavior, it is clear that the central banks did not adequately understand their audience. And it was clear that their audience's wishes, hopes, and concerns did not reach the deliberations of policymakers.

To be sure, central bankers know that they need to understand the real economy better. For this reason, they send staff out to interview small-business owners around their countries and give speeches to academic and industry groups. At the Bank of Japan, new recruits are usually posted to branch offices in provincial areas, where they cut their teeth on informal interviews with small-business owners. The aim is to understand the real economy from the ground up.

Unfortunately, such conversations become far less frequent as policymakers move up the chain of command. These officials routinely speak at meetings of academics and financial market executives. Yet they are less comfortable with, and less likely to speak to, local property owners, small-business owners, labor unions, NGO groups, consumer organizations, and others who also have a legitimate stake in the political economy. Mrs. Watanabe does not usually get invited, nor does she have much interest in attending these events. The points of view of such groups are too often modeled rather than solicited. Engaging the public is not a high priority on the central banker's to-do list, nor is it a skill he or she has worked carefully to hone.

Addressing this cultural divide between central bankers and the wider public needs to become a core part of the central bank's mission, in the same way that it is already a core part of the central bank's mission to be in close touch with the staff of leading financial institutions. The new basis for central bank legitimacy will not be trust alone; it will also include central bankers' ability to show that they listen and engage. Central banks will need to demonstrate that they have concrete internal mechanisms in place for critical self-evaluation and reflection on what they have learned about how ordinary people understand the state of the market.

Communicate More Effectively

In order to achieve this kind of engagement, central bankers will need to develop new languages, frameworks, and metaphors that allow them to speak more fully and honestly to various publics, both at home and abroad. Communication with the public must now be understood as a core activity and task of central banks—not something secondary to policymaking, but the very stuff of policymaking.

This requires first understanding the knowledge gaps of the public and addressing them. For example, at a recent Cornell conference, one central banker pointed out that people intuitively understand national economies in terms of their own household economies and do not appreciate that what might be best for the household economy, such as constraining spending in favor of saving, can be devastating for the national economy. Here is a specific but crucial detail of public education—something of a different order from the "forward guidance" that we normally associate with central bank communications. Identifying such kernels and devising strategies to change the public debate is crucial to the quality of our democratic process.

Central bankers must also learn to work with a more diverse swath of media than the usual mainstream financial press, and with far greater sophistication, if they wish to get ahead of the falsehoods and conspiracies that proliferate with lack of understanding. Olav Velthuis, an anthropologist who has studied interactions between central bankers at the European Central Bank and the journalists who cover the ECB, finds that central bankers have a fundamentally different understanding of the nature and purpose of those interactions than journalists do. The central bankers think of encounters with journalists as simply opportunities to release information, and have little understanding of the social and institutional pressures under which journalists produce stories. "The ECB sees the media as a neutral transmission tool for information released by the bank itself (a view which has obviously long been abandoned in academic studies of how the media actually operate, in favour of some sort of constructionist view of the media),” Velthius notes.[8] As a result, central bankers are often surprised and disappointed with the way their communications play as news stories.

Too often, public officials' idea of a conversation with the public involves simplifying or dumbing down.[9] They assume that nonexperts cannot understand the true messiness of the picture. But David Archer argues that the story central bankers have told the public is far too simple, not too complex, and hence is getting them into trouble. The focus of the discussion with the public has been largely limited to managing inflation. He argues that this seriously understates the complexity of the task of central bankers; it is simply not a fair description of what "financial stability" means. For example, it does not include the stability of the financial intermediation system nor, indeed, other economic indicators of financial stability: "The fundamental problem is the difficulty in describing how we would use far-reaching transactional and regulatory powers to maintain 'financial stability.' We cannot yet describe with any clarity how delegated powers of the state would be used efficiently and fairly to achieve an end that we can only, for now, describe in the negative—the absence of crises, or worst of all the absence of 'too much' instability."[10]

Of course, to say that the discussion must be complex and open to acknowledging ambiguity does not mean that a discussion with the public takes place in the same registers as a discussion with colleagues within the central bank community or with market participants. Other registers for dialogue—equally sophisticated registers—must be found and cultivated. Yet, as Archer suggests, the issue here is not just how to communicate, but what central banks communicate about. It has become well accepted among central bankers that it is important to communicate one's monetary policy so as to create expectations among investors and encourage them to make choices in line with the policy. This is clearly important. Yet it does nothing for the problem of a cultural divide between experts and publics, nor does it facilitate the public's exercise of its financial citizenship rights and duties. Rather, what is needed is communication about the dilemmas, the gray areas, the trade-offs, and the value judgments.

At a recent meeting of central bankers and their usual interlocutors among the financial press and the academy I attended, one well-known financial journalist brought up a recent pronouncement by the governor of the People's Bank of China (PBOC). The governor had stated that without intervention from the PBOC, China may soon face a "Minsky Moment"—a moment at which inflated asset prices collapse. In a remarkable example of how captured by the central bankers' culture a journalist can be, this journalist (who one might think would be in favor of as much free communication by policymakers as possible) dismissed the PBOC governor's comments as unwise and perhaps even reckless. We obviously do not want central bankers being that honest with the public, he said, suggesting that loose lips sink markets. Yet why is it necessarily a "mistake" on the part of a high-level policymaker to engage with the public honestly about the dangers ahead and the possible limitations of available tools to address them? In fact, the days and weeks that followed showed that the governor's comment did not cause markets to collapse. But it did perhaps provide in its example an opening, an avenue for a more substantive and serious dialogue—something beyond a tool to manipulate the market with words.

Beyond this there is also need for a more substantive conversation about the political or institutional issues at stake in the reach of central banks' powers. There is a need for conversation about the role of the public, the executive branch, and the legislature in economic governance, as well as about the wider political implications and purposes of central banking. In this area obviously the purpose of communication is for the central bank to learn as much as to educate. It needs to understand the public mood and to understand better what different segments of society want of the central bank.

Doug Holmes argues that many central bankers are, in fact, aware that if they want to claim to operate on behalf of the public, they must be in constant communication with it, and that their policies must be "legible" to the public. He argues that ECB communications aim to engage directly with the politics of the moment and play a part in the outcomes. Holmes writes of currencies as "public" in the sense that central bankers understand that in order for monetary policy to work, "the public broadly must be recruited to collaborate with central banks in achieving the ends of monetary policy."[11] For those central bankers, monetary policy is a collaboration with the public, and one with larger political goals. Yet although some central bankers think in visionary terms about the wider purposes of communication, beyond simply moving the market, this view of communications as a constructive political project is not part of the standard training of most central bankers. There is room for greater mainstreaming of these ideas.

In sum, one of the implications of the changing politics of central banking is that central bankers now must consider it part of their job description to reach out far beyond their own epistemic community. We need to begin to view the very project of financial governance as a collaboration with consumers/citizens/workers, just as policymakers already regard it as a collaboration with leading market participants. This, in turn, will require financial regulators to become more open to other points of view beyond the community of experts with whom they feel most comfortable. They will have to come to terms with how their own expert culture limits their interest in, and ability to hear, other points of view. Central bankers should be constantly seeking out opportunities to share the true nature of the choices they must make with a broader range of interest groups. They need to cultivate these contacts and to see it as their task to educate, communicate, and also learn. Partnerships with the academy (with individual academics and academic institutions) beyond the usual group of experts who are part of the expert culture, and with members of the NGO community, can be particularly useful here.

Explore the Possibilities of Existing Techniques

But while we are exploring new imperatives and approaches, we should not forget about the old ones. As we already discussed,[12] central bankers have a variety of tools for managing market participants' behavior—for governing. Some of these are policies and practices of communication with market insiders and the public at large. Others are technical policies, practices, and hardware in systems such as the clearing system. Others are accounting devices. There are many creative ways to deploy and redeploy these tools to shape the politics of central banking.

A most interesting recent example of such a political tool is the "stress test." After the financial crisis, it has become standard practice to require financial institutions to model what would happen to them in a case of market "stress." The test is developed and executed collaboratively between the financial institution and the policymakers, and a summary of the results is made publicly available. This exercise is an excellent opportunity for regulators to prod market participants to think more about certain issues (and perhaps less about others) and also to communicate with the public about the state of the microeconomy, if the public is paying attention.

These mundane technical tricks of the trade are tools for navigating the political moment. Through the clever deployment of such techniques, the most skilled central bankers manage the question of central bank legitimacy. But these techniques are not usually discussed as tools for addressing the politics of central banking. It remains, then, to think hard about the possible new uses of these old tools. For example, how can they be used to diffuse a more dangerous populist politics and channel it into a more productive, collaborative political relationship with the citizenry?

Expand the Toolbox

In addition to existing techniques, anthropological and sociological research tools are key to framing a new account of central bank legitimacy. The current quantitative consumer survey provides one kind of information about consumer moods. But what is needed is something much broader and more subtle: insight about new ways of communicating with the public, and most of all a new explanation for the significance of the central bank in economic and political life. Civil society institutions from the economic press to the NGO community have a critical role to play.

Since the crisis of 2008, and even long before, many scholars and policymakers, dismayed by the impact of neoclassical economics, have turned away from neoclassical theories of markets[13]—embracing Keynesian theories of markets over neoclassical ones. Yet few have been willing to seriously supplement economic analysis with other analytical tools for making sense of markets. But economics (like all disciplines) ignores certain aspects of reality in order to focus on others. In particular, it lacks a framework for understanding the nature of politics, of culture, and of regulation. For this we need new tools.

If policymakers are to engage the politics of central banking they will need to develop expertise in methodologies that allow them to understand, talk about, and respond to this politics in a sophisticated way. If our goal is to understand the culture of central banking, we must expand the range of methodologies and disciplines to accommodate fields that have longstanding expertise with cultural phenomena. If central banks are cultural actors, sophisticated tools from the disciplines of law, political economy, sociology, anthropology, and the humanities can help us understand the political effects of central bank policies as well as national and international controversies over central bank independence.

Political scientists and political economists, with their focus on "the institutional configurations of contemporary capitalism,"[14] can help us to ask a number of new and important questions: Who are the beneficiaries of central bank policies, and who are the losers? How and why do certain actors come to be supported by central banks? How does domestic politics—the actions of elected officials, the impact of electoral politics, and the place of citizens' movements and of political interest groups—affect global finance and its regulation?[15] Likewise, political theorists can help us to ask normative questions: What kind of ethical or political obligations do experts owe to the public? What kinds of distributional inequalities should be tolerated in the name of aggregate economic welfare? "Nonorthodox" economic theories can provide alternative lenses for understanding the politics of economic relations. Historical and comparative analyses provide important sources of alternative ideas and comparative perspectives on the present.

Our still rather amateurish understanding of the reception of central bank communications would benefit from far greater anthropological and sociological research. Borrowing from a sophisticated linguistic approach known as speech act theory, a number of scholars have shown how market truths or givens—from the rationality of economic actors to public trust in national currencies—are made true by the way they are "performed." Such performances include institutional arrangements, the widespread usage of certain economic theories, and the carefully crafted public statements of government officials.[16] "The insight of this research," according to sociologists Carruthers and Kim, "is that we should not simply ask if the model was accurate or not. Rather, we should study how the model was enacted, applied, or performed so that it could become more or less true."[17]

Central bankers also need access to other methods for studying ordinary people's perceptions of the economy. Journalist and anthropologist Gillian Tett recently said of a speech by Fed chair Janet Yellen, "The most thought-provoking part of the speech . . . was when the Fed chair admitted to being 'baffled' by inflation expectations,"[18] that is, by the fact that ordinary people out there were not reading the economy in the way Yellen thought they should. Tett suggests that if the Fed finds ordinary people baffling, perhaps they should consider deploying sophisticated tools for *asking* those people what they are thinking, rather than simply modeling their thoughts using economic models of what they "should" be thinking. One important element of qualitative sociological and anthropological research is the commitment to long-term participant observation in environments such as financial markets. Anthropologists of finance gather data through extensive, repeated, wide-ranging conversations with regulators and market participants, and they supplement what insiders say about finance with observations of what these groups actually do. This is often done through case studies that stretch over several years or more. As sociologist Carlo Tognato argues, central bankers will need to have access to the state of the art on matters of ritual, narrative, and symbolism and their relation to national identity to understand the central bank's place in the changing cultural politics of the moment and how their actions and communications influence cultural politics.[19]

The expert culture of central banking itself likewise can be better understood using tools from critical social theory, sociology, and anthropology that illuminate "how economic outcomes depend on the structure of social networks, institutional configurations, and cultural frames."[20] For example, in the sociology of markets there has been a lively debate about how "rational expectations"—the mainstay of economic analysis of markets—are socially formed in the context of particular social networks that shape what is expected and what is rational.[21] These methods help us to understand more precisely how policymakers' and market participants' membership in an epistemic community—fostered by similar educational backgrounds and inculcation in a particular set of economic theories—limits collective understanding of problems and limits creativity in identifying solutions.[22]

In sum, the range of social phenomena central bankers need to understand to do their job in the current environment goes far beyond inflation expectations per se. The events prior to and since 2008 are symptomatic of deeper social, political, and epistemological shifts in global society. Policymakers need to navigate this uncertainty by developing the ability to take the pulse of the intellectual and cultural climate and to gauge its political implications with far more sophistication and speed.

The dominant paradigms we have used to make sense of our economies—from scientific paradigms that emphasize the predictability of future action based on the rationality of human motivations, to assumptions about what makes states or markets politically legitimate—are under profound pressure. They may even be in the process of crumbling. In a complex world, multiple forms of expertise are needed to shape and communicate public policy. However, to date, such approaches are woefully underrepresented inside central banks.[23]

Institutional Implications

What can central banks do to ensure that this conversation with the public becomes a priority? First, and most simply, whenever central banks hold policy conferences, participants should include not just representatives of the big banks and professors, but representatives of NGOs and consumer groups. In my experience attending such conferences around the world, such groups are almost never represented. Second, research shows that greater geographical and demographic diversity among the employees of an institution can help to bring a wider range of points of view to the table. It is encouraging to see central banks beginning to promote many highly qualified women to senior and midlevel positions. Even more could be done to hire more graduates from a broader range of universities and with training in disciplines other than economics or law, and to increase the number of foreign employees, particularly those from underrepresented geographical areas such as rural communities within each bank.

One criticism of the project I have laid out—for a deep and broad engagement with the public—that one sometimes hears from central bankers comes from a particular reading of a political science literature known as public choice theory. According to this strange and counterintuitive argument, since central bankers are rational self-interested human beings, they make policy choices to maximize their individual self-interest. For this reason, they are, according to public choice theory, prone to being "captured" by the constituencies that fund them (most logically, the large banks where they can find employment after public service). Therefore, following the public choice theory argument, they cannot be trusted to engage with the public directly or to interpret the public's wishes since they will inevitably just do what serves their narrow self-interest. Rather, it should be up to elected officials alone to engage with the public. After all, it is arguably in elected officials' rational self-interest to do what the public wants, or they will be voted out of office.

There are many things wrong with this twisted argument against public engagement. First, and most obviously, an argument that central bankers cannot be trusted to act in the public interest becomes an argument against more public accountability. It becomes an argument not to engage with the public at all. Second, the problem is that central bankers are already in close contact with the one interest group that public choice theory would suggest is most likely to capture them: the leaders of the financial markets. They meet with them regularly at conferences, briefings, in one-on-one meetings, even in social settings. And yet no one is proposing that these contacts be eliminated. Empirical studies show that economic elites and organized groups representing business interests "have substantial independent impact on US government policy." The same studies show that citizens and mass-based interest groups do not have similarly substantial independent influence.[24] Given that central bankers are already engaged with one important interest group, public choice theory itself would advocate more engagement with other interest groups as well. Third, public choice theory has been criticized in recent years for its oversimplistic model of agency and motivation. Bureaucrats' preferences cannot be nakedly reduced to their personal pecuniary or political interests. There are many cases of people acting for the benefit of some larger good. Even more importantly, how bureaucrats define either their own personal interests or the wider societal good is the product of cultural, political, and ideological frames—what in this book we have been calling culture—and these frames can change over time through interaction with a new range of actors. For all these reasons, there is no basis to an argument that it is somehow improper for central bankers to engage more directly with the public and try to understand what different sectors of society expect from them.

Citizens' Obligations

The cultural rift that separates policymakers from the people who make up the so-called real economy cannot be repaired from one side alone. Citizens also have a duty to challenge policymakers constructively, to help rethink the givens by bringing new perspectives into the discussions, and to engage with hope rather than cynicism or desperation.

While the financial industry clearly understands its interest in what central banks do and invests in making its views heard by regulators, the public is far less engaged with the details of monetary policy or financial regulation. There is surprisingly little involvement and attention from the public, compared to issues such as health care and free trade. Central banks and their policies may seem far from the ordinary person's experience. It is easy for most of us to imagine that we have nothing to contribute to the debate about what central banks should do.

In fact, almost everything central banks do has one ultimate target, one ultimate audience and testing point—the citizen/consumer. For example, the U.S. financial crisis of 2008 began with problems in the ordinary domestic housing market caused by perverse and in some cases downright fraudulent consumer lending practices on the part of some banks—as well as perverse and in some cases downright fraudulent borrowing practices on the part of some consumers. In other words, the financial crisis began with economic activity in places like Florida and Nevada, not in Washington, D.C., or New York City. One of the reasons for the crisis was the conceptual disconnect between Nevada and New York that made it possible for financial intermediaries to conceal and for policymakers to be ignorant about the actual state of the so-called real economy.

So much of the popular writing about financial regulation is highly cynical in nature. Commentators score a quick hit on their websites or a retweet from their Twitter accounts by railing against experts as corrupt, incompetent individuals. Not only are most central bankers not partisan, but many of them share some of the citizenry's core concerns about financial regulation. Many central bankers are in fact highly critical of the motivations of large financial players and concerned about the economic welfare of ordinary citizens. There is more room for dialogue across our cultural differences than we might expect.

Railing against the experts, as many popular commentators do, is, in fact, a strategy of weakness. It is something one does when one thinks one has no power, no chance, no right to be fully at the table. But trashing the experts does not improve ordinary people's welfare. What we need are new, creative solutions, shaped by better information and buttressed by a more inclusive and democratic politics.

A more productive conversation between citizens and experts demands that citizens too meet the experts half way. First, citizens need to accept that global interdependence is a fact that cannot be wished away. There is no returning to a world in which currencies do not fluctuate in value in relationship to one another. We cannot disentangle ourselves from the financial markets. Financial integration is a reality. It cannot be undone. What citizens need to do therefore is to demand policies from our governments and central banks that address the inequalities this system creates. In the case of globalization, this can be done, for example, by creating new taxes, subsidies, and social programs to alleviate the unfair burdens of globalization. It can be done by working to build political coalitions across borders, or by developing programs with the people in faraway places who—as a consequence of globalization—become our allies. In the case of monetary policy, we can demand that central banks pay greater attention to employment and inequality. Where employment and inequality are not explicitly part of central banks' mandates, we can lobby legislatures to include them. We can begin to ask questions about what central banks are purchasing when they engage in quantitative easing policies in order to ensure that these purchases benefit a wider range of societal interests.

Second, in order to exercise our financial citizenship rights for the greater common good, we need to pay attention to and care about the details of financial policymaking. For example, technical rule changes that the U.S. Congress is considering to the Dodd-Frank legislation will have a substantial impact on our everyday lives. Lobbyists and politicians are banking on the fact that ordinary people will find all this far too boring to pay attention to.

We have to care about the technicalities, however, because the difficult trade-offs are buried in the technical detail. We need to make financial regulatory policy a theme of electoral politics. We need to demand a discussion of the distributive consequences of specific rule changes. We need to demand involvement in dialogue about the implications of rule changes for who would be left responsible in the case of a financial crisis and for how ordinary people would be affected. We need to ask questions about how specific policy details influence the ordinary person's ability to get a loan, or save for their kids' education, or find employment. We need to ask about how these details impact people elsewhere who have no voice in our domestic, democratic deliberations.

That said, we must also insist on the fact that finance is not all about technicalities. It is also about real people's livelihoods and about cultural preferences and ways of doing things that the financial experts are most definitely *not* experts about. What goes on in the larger society and in the wider political sphere influences financial governance. The stories that are told in our cultures about the economy—how it works, why it works the way it does—and its relationship to our identity as citizens impact which policy choices seem preferable or even plausible. These stories originate outside of central banks and, indeed, outside of the circles of the financial elite. We, the public, write these stories, alongside politicians, the media, the academy, and the wider cultural institutions such as film, literature, and the arts.

Thinking about financial governance as both local and global has dramatic consequences for the nature of citizen engagement with central banks. Citizens in one locale may find that they have interests in common with similarly situated people in other parts of the world, as new information technologies make it possible for them to organize across borders, distances, languages, and cultural barriers to advocate for our common interests. We may come to appreciate how the actions of domestic or foreign financial actors outside our national boundaries have effects on our lives—and we may wish to address these effects through advocacy to international organizations, and in foreign countries, as well as before our own domestic government, courts, and bureaucracies. Finally, we may find that in order to understand what is happening in our own communities, or to imagine what policies we might want, we need to learn from what is happening or has happened elsewhere. Comparative analysis needs to be a part of the citizen's toolkit.

Once citizens recognize the significance of the information we hold, collectively, about the nature of the real economy, and how a breakdown in communication among policymakers, financial market participants, and "the real economy" can produce devastating outcomes for the lives of ordinary people, we can begin to think about how to aggregate our information to make it accessible to policymakers and get our voices heard. We can begin by reframing consumers', citizens', and workers' points of view as forms of expertise that must be a part of the policy discussions for the sake of our collective economic welfare.

A Role for Academics

In the academic study of financial regulation prior to 2008, the only serious perspective was the viewpoint of the banks and dealers, or perhaps, on occasion, one of the large institutional investors.[25] Although financial products were marketed to the public prior to the financial crisis, end consumers or their views were rarely part of the academic debate. Ordinary people's views, it was assumed, could simply be modeled based on an understanding of how any standard rational economic actor might behave. At an academic conference devoted to central banking policy circa 2000, you would very rarely encounter a representative of an NGO, and the idea of engaging directly with members of the public in academic scholarship would have seemed somewhat silly.

Since 2008, however, we are beginning to accept that the perspective of ordinary citizens and consumers about the policies that affect them is also relevant. Academics and policymakers alike now appreciate, for example, that consumer finance and household debt are "macro-relevant"—that they can lead to systemic instability. The increasing room for appointment of economists with backgrounds in fields such as labor economics to the Federal Reserve Board, already begun prior to the crisis, institutionalizes this now mainstream view.[26] Yet insufficient attention is still being paid to the perspectives of consumers, citizens, and civil society groups: How do they interpret or misinterpret central bank actions and communications? What larger impact do these actions have on the political process? How are their lives affected by central bank actions?

The necessary next step is to inquire, in serious and rigorous scholarly detail, into the experiences of ordinary people of all backgrounds with economic and financial instruments from securities to housing to employment contracts, and to look at financial regulation and financial crisis from the vantage point of ordinary people. Already, this perspective is bringing into view dramatic disparities in access to credit. And it is revealing how the labor market impact of the financial downturn post-2008 depended on one's income, one's race, and the region in which one lives.[27] Further work will help us to bridge the gap between policy insiders and the public at large by bringing the voices and experiences of the wider society into the academic discussion. Studying the public's relationship to financial markets should be a central focus of scholarship.

Academics also still too rarely think of the global public as an *audience* for their work, on par with policymakers. They do not understand the special role they have to play in bridging the divide between policymakers and the public, and hence in addressing the political crisis surrounding the politics of expertise. They have too often been bought into the worldview in which the nonexpert point of view is most often irrelevant or misguided. By virtue of their experience in the classroom bringing young people without technical backgrounds into the expert world, however, academics stand to provide much-needed leadership in staging and guiding a policy conversation across the cultural divide between experts and publics. Anthropologists have particular expertise here because their key method, ethnography, entails listening across cultural differences and making sense of the assumptions and views of one community to another.

There is also a need for much more comparative analysis. Within the neoclassical view of markets, any differences between markets were simply the product of "irrationalities" and would eventually disappear. But once we abandon the neoclassical economic view of markets as inherently rational and self-regulating, we must also assume that markets are not the same everywhere.[28] These differences are not just a result of culture, but of historical and present-day inequalities. These inequalities are highlighted as soon as we begin to ask questions such as "What does the global financial regulatory system look like from the perspective of countries outside the North Atlantic consensus?"[29] or "How could such countries play a larger role in international financial governance?"

And yet thinking about these differences turns out to be quite a tricky matter. First, it takes careful and sensitive observation to tease them out because although markets are constituted by globally circulating ideas, experts, and funds, there are sometimes imperceptible differences among markets. At the same time, it is easy to overstate differences, and "alternatives" to global capitalism often turn out to be less alternative than meets the eye.[30] For example, Islamic finance positions itself as very distinct from global capitalism but turns out to be a highly rational set of financial practices integrated in complex ways into dominant financial markets.[31]

A Role for the Media

The financial media is a crucial player in the relationship between financial experts and the public and has a critical role to play in the amelioration of that relationship. For a long time, the financial press has exhibited the same biases as academics. They have been oriented toward the experts and the financial market leaders, and have reflected those people's point of view. The financial press and the financial markets have enjoyed a highly symbiotic relationship. Financial market leaders and financial regulators use the financial media to speak to one another. For example, in my research I have encountered many occasions on which financial market insiders encouraged stories in the *Financial Times* concerning the need for a particular regulation or deregulation in hopes of spurring regulators to act. For this very reason, these same people provide a market for the financial news media. This media becomes mandatory reading inside the central banks and inside the financial firms.

Of course, journalists and central bankers have different incentives and different interests. Journalism is a highly competitive business, and the pressures to be read and respected by the mainstream financial elites are intense. Moreover, the complexity of finance can also be intimidating to journalists, experts can be trusted sources, and it is sometimes hard to have confidence that the experts can be wrong, or that something the experts regard as irrelevant is nevertheless central to the story.

Since the financial crisis we have seen an important shift in the perspective of the financial media. Many journalists have become far more critical of the financial markets' internal perspective, and many more stories in the mainstream financial press take a position that is more pro-regulation. Regulators have become highly trusted sources of information about the financial markets alongside financial market participants. And yet we still see relatively little engagement with ordinary people as sources or subjects of financial reporting. The audience and sourcing for financial journalism has become a bit larger but still is a highly elite group.

Given the economics of journalism, and the fact that the most popular pages of national newspapers remain its sports pages, not its financial pages, this is perhaps understandable. And yet the proliferation of citizen journalism and fringe online media writing about financial governance suggests nonetheless that there is a much larger audience for financial news out there. Journalists need to reach this audience with material that educates and illuminates, that provides the context for the policy debate people need to engage, or fringe conspiracy theorists will do the job instead.

One way journalists can do this is to educate themselves about what might interest the larger public by engaging a wider range of sources for stories about financial governance. It is encouraging to see many more stories about the impact (positive and negative) of financial markets on ordinary people in places far away from New York and London. Yet even when the story is not about "life on Main Street," there is a role for a wider range of sources than the traditional experts. Of course, identifying these sources requires judgment, confidence, and courage, not to mention time. Yet, as the media comes to reflect a wider range of cultural points of view it can help to educate all of these cultures about one another.

A New Dialogue between Experts and Publics

One important problem remains: As Dimity Kingsford-Smith and Olivia Dixon write, "There are few avenues for expressing collective political and social values about financialized welfare provision rather than investors' economic valuations. If financial citizens are to move away from pure democratic action (such as the 'Occupy Wall Street' movement) or individual financial valuation at the other extreme, then they must institutionalize."[32] We lack the organizations and institutions that can enable ordinary people to organize and express their collective views about matters of financial governance in dialogue with experts.

We must now find ways to stage and sustain such a serious and creative dialogue—one that is transformative of the relationship between experts and nonexperts. It must be a collaborative effort across the boundaries of the academy, government, the private sector, and civil society. In my view, the design and implementation of this dialogue is among the most pressing issues now facing scholars, activists, and policymakers.

Concretely, what is needed is a new kind of institutional arrangement, or platform, for engagement, across barriers of nation-states but also across the cultural divides that separate experts and nonexperts, government officials and civil society. This platform must be both able to accommodate broad normative and ethical questions and able to address specialized technical issues. It must make room for a diversity of points of view and for agendas driven from the bottom up, yet it must also be managed and results-driven. It must be engineered to enable persons of different linguistic, social, economic, scholarly, and political vantage points to usefully input into the process. The difficult challenge is how to create a platform for policymaking

that is both inclusive, on the one hand, and also able to tackle specific technical questions with precision and sophistication, on the other hand. Yet what
would such a platform look like? All of our existing institutional options for
policy formulation presuppose a conversation among experts.

Over the past five years, I have been experimenting with a prototype for
this kind of platform. Meridian 180, a multilingual platform for policy ex-
perimentation and innovation,[33] brings together more than 800 policymakers, industry representatives, academics, and representatives of civil society
from thirty-nine countries. Meridian 180 operates around a model for policy dialogue that aims to be at once open and yet able to produce precise and
technical policy innovation. The organizational structure is a hybrid of an
international membership organization and a federation of universities.
As in an international membership organization, policymakers and representatives of civil society participate as private individuals and then feed
ideas and solutions to their own institutions, communities, and networks.
And as in a federation of universities, resources, links to national policymakers, university presses, and intellectual talent pools are shared across
national boundaries. Problems are framed for dialogue from the ground
up by local clusters of participants, but then filtered through a refining process using online discussions, live meetings, more sustained working groups,
and ultimately distribution channels such as think tanks and university
presses. This book is in fact an outcome of this process. The Meridian 180
experience may be useful for beginning to articulate some of the necessary
features of a dialogue between citizens and experts. What follows are a set of
institutional features that, in my view, are critical.

I. THE PLATFORM MUST BE INCLUSIVE AND DIVERSE

Representatives of different national linguistic, social, economic, scholarly,
professional, and political vantage points must be engaged. The goal here
must be to ensure that the widest possible range of critiques of financial governance policies is brought in and addressed at early stages so that agreements do not find themselves exposed to fundamental outside critiques at
the final stage.

It will be crucial to ensure that participation by both interest groups and
individuals is possible. At the idea incubation stage we need the unfiltered
participation of individuals, and not just of political entrepreneurs. Aca-

demics are of course one important group of individual idea generators, but thought leaders outside of formal academic institutions must be engaged as well.

A key feature of the Meridian 180 experiment is that corporate interests, nation-states, and even civil society groups are only informally represented in the discussions by people who participate in their individual capacities (albeit with an understanding that their point of view is shaped by the networks and institutions they represent). The rationale is that in order for new ideas to emerge (not to mention for new social ties across existing fault lines to emerge) we need to preserve some space for risk taking and free play. Participants need the freedom to experiment with ideas, and the time out from the burden of "representing" their institution or constituency to become curious about ideas different from their own.

How should participants be selected? The most democratic means is self-selection. Ideally, we should devise a system in which participation at succeeding higher levels of engagement is made available based on individuals' demonstrated commitment to participate in a serious and sustained way. Participation should also be based more on a participant's ability to garner the support and respect of others at the table than on expert qualifications. This is the model of participation in local politics in many places; the challenge is how to scale the experience of local politics up. In Meridian 180, we have found that a self-selection model produces remarkable quality and commitment; those around the table are engaged because they want to be. They find satisfaction and excitement in meeting other equally engaged individuals from very different backgrounds. Contrary to the collective wisdom that the very best people must be enticed with financial rewards, we have found that the quality of the participants who choose to devote themselves out of pure commitment to and love of the project of idea generation is remarkably high.

Leadership in such a large and diverse group requires a tiered system of committees with successively larger degrees of responsibility. To preserve opportunity of access, membership in the lowest-ranking committees should be open to all (subject to certain geographical and knowledge quotas with choices made by lottery and waiting lists). Yet in order to ensure quality of result, committees at all levels can deploy a collaborative means of ranking or scoring the value of participation other than by institutional affiliation or educational pedigree. For example, individual participation in the committee structure could be subject to 360 degree review by other participants. Individuals with the highest rankings could advance to leadership roles, while individuals with consistently low ratings could be dropped from further rounds of discussion. Of course this is only one institutional proposal. The point, however, is that unlike existing institutional arrangements, serious design attention must be given to ensuring both access and quality of participation.

2. DIALOGUE METHODOLOGY MUST ENABLE PARTICIPATORY DISCUSSION

A second challenge is to devise a structure that enables serious deliberation on specific policy issues while ensuring that the issues are not already framed by expert perspectives in ways that exclude legitimate outside concerns.

How to ensure meaningful diverse and inclusive participation is of course a great challenge. Ten years ago, such a conversation would have seemed impossible. The logistical hurdles were insurmountable. But participatory democracy experts agree that new information technologies, along with the increasingly widespread availability of those technologies even in the developing world, open up new possibilities: "Today technology permits knowledge to bubble up from more dispersed sources that are filtered through more competitive mechanisms, sustaining a more decentralized and accurate system of social discovery. We can acquire general expertise without being beholden to particular experts."[34] Technology allows us to eliminate unnecessary barriers to participation (in particular expensive travel costs associated with meetings, and linguistic barriers), and artificial intelligence and crowd-sourcing translation technologies enable ideas to be bundled, weighted according to their degree of support, and edited collectively.

In Meridian 180 we have addressed the challenge of maintaining a very specific technical focus while remaining open to outside points of view by staging multiple rounds of discussions, with shifting groups of participants depending on the scope or stage of the discussion. An initial grouping of participants engaged in online brainstorming over a relatively short period of time generate a series of questions to be addressed separately and with greater technical precision by smaller groups of participants with specific knowledge or experience. The results of those technical deliberations can then be fed back into the larger group discussions or may lead to further proposals or ideas to be taken up by other smaller groupings. We follow a process of multiple refinements of the positions through dialogue between the various groups, in successive versions. This refinement is linked to a rigorous self-evaluation procedure in which participants determine whether individual participants and the group as a whole are on the right track. This process allows ideas to emerge from the ground up. The key is that any idea for discussion that garners a substantial threshold of collective interest must be given a chance to float a trial balloon, with the appreciation that most of these trial balloons should and will fail.

This process is admittedly longer and more cumbersome than existing approaches to policymaking. Yet it is important to remember that the process has two goals, and not simply one. The first goal, of course, is to generate agreement on financial governance policy, but the second and equally important goal is to build social ties across cultural barriers. What may seem like wasted effort from the standpoint of the first goal may be precisely the engine of progress from the standpoint of the second goal.

3. MULTIPLE OUTCOMES

If the goal is not simply to write policy but to stage a cultural shift, we should seek to create as porous as possible a barrier between the world of the deliberations and the world of implementation. Here, the participants in the deliberations come to serve a different function: they have been brought into the process not simply because of their knowledge but also because of their social ties. It is they who must take the ideas that emerge from the discussions and bring them forward for discussion and action in the other settings in which they find themselves, the other political sites in which they act. For example, academics might begin writing about these issues, teaching about them, or spearheading new university partnerships. Activists might find uses for these ideas and hence become champions for them in their own local, regional, or international campaigns. And central bankers might champion policy proposals internally. The idea is that rather than one conduit to policy, a myriad such conduits, each with their own backers and constituencies, open up. In this way the social dimension of the exercise becomes the engine of exponential increases in power and legitimacy.

Universities, colleges, and technical schools, as well as independent think tanks, have an especially important role to play both in recruiting participants and in staging these conversations. Existing networks of elite and community-based education and policy analysis within nations and across national borders could serve as an important institutional backbone. Academic institutions and research-oriented think tanks provide a safe space of reason and deliberation, a commitment to political neutrality, and a focus on the long-term and larger context necessary for a conversation between experts and the publics to succeed.

CONCLUSION

Between the Last Financial Crisis and the Next One

The financial crisis of 2008 is now receding from view. It is no longer in the daily newspaper headlines. Although the economic consequences—particularly for the distribution of wealth—are very much still with us, public attention seems to be elsewhere. In the United States, the Trump administration and Congress are pushing for a substantial repeal of the Dodd-Frank regulations put in place to try to prevent or at least lessen the impact of the next financial crisis.

Nevertheless, another financial crisis is on the horizon. We know this, although we are unsure about the precise details of the timing or the origin of the contagion. And we know this *in spite of* the policymakers' models, which still assume that financial crises are extraordinary or unlikely events.

As with the crisis of 2008, the impact will most likely be global and pervasive. Ordinary citizens will pay a heavy price, just as they did in 2008. Retirement savings accounts will experience losses. Homes will be worth less than before. Jobs will be at risk. Many workers may be forced, once again, to endure cuts to wages or benefits. In the developing world, the consequences may be more extreme.

When the next financial crisis occurs, governments will once again have to face a choice: Should taxpayer funds be used to bail out financial institutions? Should central banks once again inject large amounts of cash into the economy through the banks? Should central banks purchase the assets and debts of private companies to keep them afloat? These are not just technical questions but normative questions. As David Archer, head of Central Bank Studies at the Bank for International Settlements, argues, such choices also precipitate a "coming crisis of legitimacy": "Central banks are showing a strong inclination to use powers that they already have, or could be argued to have, for new, imperfectly-defined purposes. It is this reinterpretation of the proper use of delegated state powers that threatens legitimacy."[1]

As Peter Katzenstein has suggested, the next crisis will be far more politically complex than the last one. The speed and velocity of contemporary politics is simply much greater than it was then. Having developed a narrative of popular outrage against elites, the public will not accept backroom bailouts and technical talk of swap lines as being in the public interest as easily as it did in 2008. Moreover, the changing nature of the media itself—in particular the rise of alternative and social media that are far more difficult for policymakers to manage—assures that the public backlash will be faster and stronger.

Given all of this, now is the time to address the legitimacy of central bank actions, the tools to be used, and the choices to be made. We must do this before the next crisis hits, through democratic processes, rather than allowing our collective response to be relegated to rushed decisions by elites behind closed doors in the panic of the moment. This is as urgent a macroprudential matter as any other on the agenda of central banks today.

In the United States, the regulatory framework introduced through Dodd-Frank was designed to prevent market participants from taking on too much risk or from cheating borrowers and investors. It was meant to force market participants to put aside enough assets to protect them in the event of a crisis, as well as to allow regulators to gather information about problems in advance so that they can hopefully be addressed before a calamity occurs. A second goal of the Dodd-Frank legislation was to ensure that the industry would create its own insurance system. It was designed to force the banks to set aside funds so that in the event of a systemic instability or failure, these funds could be used to resolve the situation without having to dip into tax coffers.

The approach of Congress was to do everything possible now to lessen the possibility of a financial crisis in the future. Or if a crisis cannot be averted, Congress hoped to reduce the cost to taxpayers by asking banks to change their practices now. So here is an example of a point at which the public has a political decision to make: changes to Dodd-Frank will have profound consequences on all of us when the next financial crisis occurs.

Financial governance involves trade-offs: benefits for some and costs for others. That makes it highly relevant to ordinary people's daily lives. The public has a right, as well as a duty, to join the conversation.

It is, of course, difficult for central banks to communicate honestly and fully with the public or the market about the possibility of crisis in advance. The fear is that any suggestion that there is even a chance of crisis will lead to an exaggerated market response that could, in fact, precipitate the kind of market downturn it seeks to avoid. Yet it is precisely this difficult, complex conversation about unknowns, second-best options, and trade-offs that desperately needs to occur among policymakers, scholars, and the public. And it must happen now.

This conversation will require more than just policy change; it will re-quire a paradigm shift. It will require new academic approaches, new re-search questions, and new policy tools. Even more than this, it will require a new kind of conversation between the experts and the public. Central bankers must now embrace a new collaborative relationship with the public because they cannot avoid it, and because they also cannot abdicate the au-thority to do it as long as elected officials have delegated to them responsibil-ity and authority for the economy. In practice, this means acknowledging the possible limitations and blind spots in one's own worldview. And it means working as hard as possible to bring other constituencies—especially the global public—into the decision-making process.

Much has been made of the question of how central bankers are ap-pointed, how long their terms should be, and what kinds of reporting re-quirements to elected officials are necessary to confer legitimacy on central banks' actions. These are important questions, but legislative oversight can-not in itself absolve central bankers of responsibility for engaging with the public, just as deference to the legislature or pure transparency regarding all central bank decisions may not be in the best interest of the public at large.

Rather, recognition that central banking is cultural, in the complex and sophisticated sense articulated here, confers on policymakers, scholars, and members of the public a responsibility to continue to communicate and to collaborate in the care for the resilience of the market, just as they would do with any important democratic institution.

Members of the public too must assume responsibility for bringing about a new kind of politics of central banking. There are many opportunities to do this. Central banks are increasingly subject to legislative oversight. Elected officials are demanding more regular briefings from central bankers and are asking for greater involvement in setting targets—and perhaps even the means of achieving those targets. One implication is that central bankers are increasingly called on to speak to the public about what they are doing. When the governor of the Bank of Japan or the chairman of the Federal Reserve testifies before the legislature, they make statements that are reported in the news media, and they are asked questions from politicians that are shaped by input from constituents and interest groups.

These briefings are opportunities for the public to engage the financial governance experts. The rise of social media and new information technologies has significantly reduced the barriers to contact with elected officials through these events. Taking advantage of this, a number of citizens' advocacy organizations have emerged since the financial crisis to counter the impact of the large financial institutions and give voice to ordinary citizens. Central bankers and regulators are highly sensitive to the responses that they receive from these encounters with the public and with legislators because the success of their interventions turns on their credibility. Many central bankers are in fact eager to engage more with the public, but lack a vehicle to do so. We can also invite central bankers to engage with our own organizations, just as they often attend meetings sponsored by the financial industry. In this way we can create opportunities for both sides to learn about one another's worldview. We can follow what central banks do in the media and engage with these policies from the point of view of on-the-ground economic and political realities through social media and the mainstream media.

A focus on cultural conflicts between experts and publics is not a panacea, of course. On the contrary, cultural analysis is by definition difficult, personal, ambiguous, and open-ended. Cultural conflicts are frustrating. Thus, one criticism of the perspective adopted in this book is that a serious engagement with cultural difference is too much to ask either of our government officials or of the public.

My response is, first, that whether we recognize it explicitly or not, we are already engaged in acts of cultural conflict—acts that have serious and lasting political and moral consequences. The issue then is, should this remain an unselfconscious, ad hoc, largely amateuristic, and arguably hegemonic exercise? Or should we confront our choices and our descriptions head on and struggle with the frustrating but ultimately important task of making our engagements in cultural conflict as sophisticated and principled as we can? The contention of this book, in other words, is that at least these are the right frustrations to have. I view this as a proposal to recognize what many central bankers are already doing, and in some areas to push to do more of this, rather than a proposal to do things entirely differently.

A second likely criticism of this proposal will come from two camps that at first blush might seem radically opposed. On the one hand, advocates of the status quo will regard my views of the expert's cultural responsibilities as far too accommodationist of popular values and concerns, and possibly even for this reason as lawless. From the opposite camp, on the other hand, the representatives of populist groups on both the right and the left may be distrustful of the possibility of honest dialogue.

I respectfully acknowledge the basis and legitimacy of these fears. Indeed, it is the fact of these fears, the fact of the "danger" of dialogue, that makes financial citizenship in conditions of culture clash so important. As the cultural theorist Ghassan Hage says, hope without fear is no hope at all. Real hope, he argues, requires that something be wagered, something be truly risked.[2]

Of course, the challenge is by no means unique to central banks. The shift to a more subtle and sophisticated relationship between experts and publics advocated here is necessary across the wider economy, the sciences, and society. How we manage this paradigm shift has profound implications not just for our economies, but for our democratic institutions as well.

ACKNOWLEDGMENTS

I am grateful to David Archer, Alan Blinder, Adam Feibelman, Anna Gelpern, Doug Holmes, Fleur Johns, Ravi Kanbur, Peter Katzenstein, Jonathan Kirshner, Erin Lockwood, Hiro Miyazaki, Kim Eric Moric, Marcelo Prates, Aditi Sahasrabuddhe, Eric San Juan, David Spence, and Gillian Tett, and to audiences at Georgetown Law School; the Behavioural Sciences and Investor Education Conference, Rio de Janeiro, Brazil; the Future of Global Finance: Populism, Technology and Regulation Conference, Columbia Law School; and the Cornell–Tel Aviv Law School Conference on the Ethics of the Market for their useful comments. I thank Liam Lawson, Tim McLellan, Aditi Sahasrabuddhe, and Lauren van Haaften-Schick for their research assistance.

Notes

1. The Legitimacy of Central Banking

1. Riles, *Collateral Knowledge*, 11–14. See also Riles, "Introduction: In Response"; and the section "A Definition of Culture" in chapter 3 of this volume.

2. Geertz, *The Interpretation of Cultures*, 3–10.

2. The Challenge to the Technocracy

1. Bank of Japan Act.

2. Goodhart, "The Evolution of Central Banks."

3. Jasanoff, "Citizens at Risk."

4. Blinder, "The Evolving Political Economy of Central Banking."

5. Posen, "Central Bank Independence after the Inflation Is Gone."

6. Alesina and Summers, "Central Bank Independence and Macroeconomic Performance."

7. Lockwood, "The Global Politics of Central Banking."

8. Posen, "Why Central Bank Independence Does Not Cause Low Inflation"; Haan and van 'T Hag, "Variation in Central Bank Independence across Countries."

9. Posen, "Central Bank Independence after the Inflation Is Gone."

10. Subbarao, *Who Moved My Interest Rate?*

11. Carvalho, "The Independence of Central Banks"; Levy, "Does an Independent Central Bank Violate Democracy?"

12. Blinder, "The Evolving Political Economy of Central Banking."

13. Posen, "Central Bank Independence after the Inflation Is Gone," 11.

14. Blinder et al., "How Do Central Banks Talk?"

15. Tucker, "The Credit Crisis."

16. Prates, "The Changing Politics of Central Banking."

17. The bill failed in the Senate by 9 votes, 53–44, on January 12, 2016.

18. Bernanke, "'Audit the Fed' Is Not about Auditing the Fed."

19. They incorrectly claim support for their position from Thomas Jefferson, who was actually making the case for an issuing bank controlled by the people as an alternative to delegating issuing power to private banking institutions.

20. Paul and Spitznagel, "The Fed Is Crippling America."

21. Paul, "Audit the Fed."

22. Sanders, "To Rein In Wall Street, Fix the Fed."

23. Sanders.

24. Sanders.

25. Quoted in Fields, "Sen. Cruz Cosponsors Rand Paul's 'Audit the Fed' Bill."

26. Bernanke, "'Audit the Fed' Is Not about Auditing the Fed."

27. Summers, "Here's What Bernie Sanders Gets Wrong—and Right—about the Fed."

28. Summers.

29. Jopson and Fleming, "Fed Challenged over Governor's Clinton Ties."

30. Quoted in Gajanan, "Federal Reserve Chair Janet Yellen Fires Back at Donald Trump over Interest Rate."

31. Reuters and Fortune Editors, "Neel Kashkari Rejects Trump's Charge That the Fed Is Beholden to Obama."

32. Quoted in Appelbaum, "Fed Official Says She Favors 'Prudence' in Raising Interest Rates."

33. Quoted in Jopson and Fleming, "Fed Challenged over Governor's Clinton Ties."

34. Blinder, "The Evolving Political Economy of Central Banking."

35. Metzger, "Through the Looking Glass to a Shared Reflection."

36. Levitin, "The Politics of Financial Regulation and the Regulation of Financial Politics," 2049–52.

37. A. Baker, "Restraining Regulatory Capture?"; Young, "Transnational Regulatory Capture?"

38. Cukierman, Webb, and Neyapti, "Measuring the Independence of Central Banks and Its Effects on Policy Outcomes."

39. Kirshner, *Monetary Orders.*

40. Mcnamara, "Rational Fictions."

41. Posen, "Central Bank Independence after the Inflation Is Gone."

42. Conti-Brown, *The Power and Independence of the Federal Reserve.*

3. The Culture of Central Banking

1. Geertz, *The Interpretation of Cultures*, 89.

2. Leach, *Custom, Law, and Terrorist Violence*, 21 ("whether we rate any particular item of behaviour as being that of a hero or a prophet, a madman or a criminal, will depend upon the context in which the judgment is made").

3. Geertz, *The Interpretation of Cultures* (arguing against the view of culture as a "super-organic").

4. Although this is sometimes described as an effect of globalization, anthropologists in fact insist that there was probably never a society in which this was not already true.

5. See Riles, "Comparative Law and Socio-legal Studies," 806.

6. Gupta and Ferguson, *Anthropological Locations*; Tsing, *Friction*; Riles, "Introduction: In Response."

7. Wagner, *The Invention of Culture*, 3.

8. Leach, *Custom, Law, and Terrorist Violence*.

9. Wagner, *The Invention of Culture*, 16.

10. Wagner.

11. Conti-Brown, *The Power and Independence of the Federal Reserve*, 13.

12. Riles, *Collateral Knowledge*.

13. Posen, "Central Bank Independence after the Inflation Is Gone."

14. Helleiner and Pagliari, "The End of an Era in International Financial Regulation?," 180.

15. For example, Stacey Steele explores how differing "bankruptcy cultures" (including both the laws and judicial institutions and social attitudes toward bankruptcy) lead to different outcomes in bankruptcy litigation involving the same clauses of the International Swaps and Derivatives Association (ISDA) master agreement brought in different jurisdictions. Steele, "The Collapse of Lehman Brothers and Derivative Disputes."

16. Riles, *Collateral Knowledge*.

17. Biggart and Beamish, "The Economic Sociology of Conventions"; cited in Katzenstein, "Panel: The Politics of Central Banking." Meg Doherty Bea in her literature review paper also develops the idea that central banks and bankers are part of a community that shares experiences and cultures. This shared background leads to similarities in the policies, strategies, and actions central banks adopt. Doherty Bea, "Constructing and Maintaining Legitimacy," 6–9.

18. Dezalay and Garth, *The Internationalization of Palace Wars*.

19. Tett, *The Silo Effect*.

20. Abbott, *The System of Professions*; Abbott, "Boundaries of Social Work or Social Work of Boundaries?"; Douglas, *How Institutions Think*; Hogle, "Introduction: Jurisdictions of Authority and Expertise."

21. See generally Tett, *The Silo Effect*; Masco, "Nuclear Technoaesthetics"; Fligstein, Brundage, and Schultz, "Seeing Like the Fed."

22. For example, in the case of efforts to develop response capacities to biothreats, Andrew Lakoff argues that the U.S. government approaches biosecurity according to a

historically specific "logic" for generating knowledge about disease drawn from the nuclear attack civil defense drills of the Cold War. Security agencies' attempts to learn which vital national infrastructures are most vulnerable and to cultivate preparedness disasters by conducting rehearsal scenarios turn out to be inadequate because the experts involved in their creation are only able to predict scenarios based on their own narrow field of expertise. These preparedness exercises have proven highly ineffective for real crises such as SARS or the East Japan earthquake where the crisis is multifaceted or could not be extrapolated from past models. See Lakoff, "From Population to Vital System."

23. Dezalay and Garth, *The Internationalization of Palace Wars.*

24. Gramsci, "The Formation of the Intellectuals."

25. Ahamed, *Lords of Finance.*

26. Stiglitz, *The Euro,* 9–10.

27. The practitioner literature is, ironically, far more agnostic about the predictive value of science than the purely academic one. Kiyohiko Nishimura argues that we should "take proper account of our intellectual limitations in modeling the real economy, and at the same time, we should be practical in coping with the many-faceted problems of financial crises." See Nishimura, "Macroprudential Lessons from the Financial Crisis," 193.

28. Holmes, *Economy of Words,* 6.

29. Holmes, 12.

30. Riles, *Collateral Knowledge.*

31. Jasanoff, *Designs on Nature*; Hogle, "Introduction: Jurisdictions of Authority and Expertise"; Wayland, "Contextualizing the Politics of Knowledge"; Cohn, "Sex and Death in the Rational World of Defense Intellectuals"; Traweek, *Beamtimes and Lifetimes.*

32. Farquhar, *Knowing Practice.* Scholars working in the Foucauldian tradition speak of expert power as both "repressive and productive" because expertise goes beyond simply compelling action; it changes the way nonexperts imagine their world and think about their options within it. Foucault, *The History of Sexuality,* vol. 1; Canguilhem and Delaporte, *A Vital Rationalist.*

33. Mitchell, *Rule of Experts.* (British colonial officers in Egypt arrogantly believed in the universal relevance of British property law.)

34. See Galeoto, Bitar, and Rudolph, "The Consumer Financial Protection Bureau," 702.

35. Hence some new work focuses on the intersection between financial regulation and consumer protection law. Ali, *Consumer Financial Dispute Resolution in a Comparative Context*; Kennedy, McCoy, and Bernstein, "The Consumer Financial Protection Bureau."

4. Culture Clash

1. Tognato, *Central Bank Independence,* 9.

2. Tognato, 3.

3. Stiglitz, *The Euro*, 35.

4. On different forms of capitalism and their political implications, see Konoe, *The Politics of Financial Markets and Regulation*.

5. C. Baker, "The Federal Reserve's Use of International Swap Lines."

6. Funke, Schularick, and Trebesch, "Going to Extremes"; quoted in Gould, "Why Is Populism Taking over the Republican Party?"

7. Tewksbury and Rittenberg, *News on the Internet*, 6.

8. Scheurer, "The Federal Reserve Is Dealing Financial Drugs."

5. Toward Financial Citizenship and a New Legitimacy Narrative

1. Anti-Defamation League, "Jewish 'Control' of the Federal Reserve: A Classic Anti-Semitic Myth."

2. In this sense, I intend something very different by "financial citizenship" than the use of the term as a "slogan by financial literacy advocates who mourn record levels of personal debt as a social failure to instill a sense of pecuniary responsibility, and proper knowledge of financial products in the public." Kear, "Governing Homo Subprimicus," 937.

3. Goodhart, "The Constitutional Position of an Independent Central Bank," 192.

4. Riles, *Collateral Knowledge*.

5. Subbarao, "G 20 and India."

6. Sørensen, "Banking on the Nation," 329.

7. Sørensen, 345.

8. I am grateful to Paul Tucker for this framing.

9. Desan, *Making Money*.

6. A Program for Action

1. Shelton, "Trump Is Right to Take Aim at the 'Political' Fed."

2. Stiglitz, *The Euro*, 153.

3. See Bytheway and Metzler, *Central Banks and Gold*.

4. Pistor, "A Legal Theory of Finance," 320.

5. Posen, "Central Bank Independence after the Inflation Is Gone"; Posen, "Why Central Bank Independence Does Not Cause Low Inflation."

6. Tucker, "The Credit Crisis."

7. Ahamed, *Lords of Finance*.

8. Velthuis, "Making Monetary Markets Transparent," 324.

9. Scholars in science and technology studies have noted and critiqued a similar set of assumptions in the way scientists engage the general public. See, e.g., Hilgartner, "The Dominant View of Popularization"; Sismondo, *An Introduction to Science and Technology Studies*, 170–74.

10. Archer, "A Coming Crisis of Legitimacy?," 86.

11. Holmes, *Economy of Words*, 1.

12. See the section "Mundane Technical Details Are Value-Laden" in chapter 3 of this volume.

13. Trachtman, "The International Law of Financial Crisis"; Kelly, "Financial Crisis and Civil Society."

14. Beckert, "Capitalism as a System of Expectations," 324.

15. See Drezner, *All Politics Is Global*, 19 and Andrews et al., "Financial Interdependence and the State," 505. ("Government leaders choose to respond to particular circumstances in particular ways; their choices are influenced by existing constellations of economic and political forces and at the same time alter (sometimes significantly) those constellations.")

16. Callon, "Introduction: The Embeddedness of Economic Markets in Economics"; see also MacKenzie, "An Equation and Its Worlds"; Lépinay, *Codes of Finance*; Power, Ashby, and Palermo, "Risk Culture in Financial Organisations"; Muniesa, "Performing Prices"; Beunza, "Tools of the Trade"; Holmes, *Economy of Words*, 4.

17. Carruthers and Kim, "The Sociology of Finance," 251.

18. Tett, "The Inflation Enigma Needs Unorthodox Answers."

19. Tognato, *Central Bank Independence*.

20. Beckert, "Capitalism as a System of Expectations," 324.

21. Social studies of finance demonstrate how "concrete social networks and relationships" are at the heart of financial institutions and arrangements from venture capital to bank loans to exchange-based trading. See Carruthers and Kim, "The Sociology of Finance," 249. The economic theory of rational expectations has been critiqued by John Maynard Keynes, who argued that expectations cannot be uniquely correct, since our existing knowledge does not provide a sufficient basis for a calculated mathematical expectation. Beckert, *Imagined Futures*, 46; quoting Keynes, *The General Theory of Employment, Interest, and Money*, 147. See also Buchanan, "The Market as a Creative Process."

22. New sociological research helps us to understand more precisely why neoclassical economics fail at this moment. Michel Callon has shown how markets become "calculable"—how the givens of mathematical calculation that make economics and hence finance work, a field of knowledge, actually depend on a quite precarious set of institutional, conceptual, and social arrangements. See Callon, "Introduction: The Embeddedness of Economic Markets in Economics," 46. ("Market laws are neither in the nature of humans and societies—waiting for the scientist, like a prince charming, to wake and reveal them—nor are they constructions or artifacts invented by social sciences in an effort to improvise simple frameworks for explaining an opaque and complex reality.") The implication is that when these sociomaterial conditions begin to shift, even in small ways, the logic and rationality of markets can quickly unravel.

23. One marginal but interesting exception: former governor of the Bank of New Zealand Arthur Grimes has engaged in amateur anthropological analysis, somewhat tongue in cheek, to reflect on the misunderstandings of central bank actions by the public. Grimes, "Monetary Policy and Economic Imbalances."

24. Gilens and Page, "Testing Theories of American Politics," 564.

25. See Warren, "The New Economics of the American Family," 1. ("Academic discourse is far too often about a forest with no trees, that is, a bankruptcy system in the abstract, unburdened by the details of real families in trouble.")

26. See, e.g., Hefeker and Neugart, "The Influence of Central Bank Transparency on Labor Market Regulation," 18.

27. Carruthers and Kim, "The Sociology of Finance," 246.

28. See Tett, *Fool's Gold*, 252. ("What social anthropology teaches its adherents is that nothing in society ever exists in a vacuum or in isolation. Holistic analysis that tries to link different parts of a social structure is crucial, be that in respect to wedding rituals or trading floors.")

29. See, e.g., Buckley, "How East Asia Could Amplify Its Voice in Global Economic Governance"; Arner and Schou-Zibell, "Asian Regulatory Responses to the Global Financial Crisis."

30. Maurer, "Resocializing Finance?," 66.

31. See, e.g., Rudnyckyj, "Economy in Practice."

32. Kingsford-Smith and Dixon, "The Consumer Interest and the Financial Markets."

33. www.meridian-180.org

34. McGinnis, *Accelerating Democracy*.

Conclusion

1. Archer, "A Coming Crisis of Legitimacy?," 86.

2. Hage, *Against Paranoid Nationalism*.

References

Abbott, Andrew Delano. "Boundaries of Social Work or Social Work of Boundaries? The Social Service Review Lecture." *Social Service Review* 69, no. 4 (1995): 545–62. https://doi.org/10.2307/30012869.

———. *The System of Professions: An Essay on the Division of Expert Labor*. Chicago: University of Chicago Press, 1988.

Ahamed, Liaquat. *Lords of Finance: The Bankers Who Broke the World*. New York: Penguin Press, 2009.

Alesina, Roberto, and Lawrence H. Summers. "Central Bank Independence and Macroeconomic Performance: Some Comparative Evidence." *Journal of Money, Credit and Banking* 25, no. 2 (1993): 151–62.

Ali, Shahla F. *Consumer Financial Dispute Resolution in a Comparative Context: Principles, Systems and Practice*. New York: Cambridge University Press, 2013. https://doi.org/10.1017/CBO9781139236829.

Andrews, David M., Thomas D. Willett, Barry Eichengreen, and Jeffry Frieden. "Financial Interdependence and the State: International Monetary Relations at Century's End." *International Organization* 51, no. 3 (1997): 479–511.

Anti-Defamation League. "Jewish 'Control' of the Federal Reserve: A Classic Anti-Semitic Myth." https://www.adl.org/resources/backgrounders/jewish-control-of-the-federal-reserve-a-classic-anti-semitic-myth.

Appelbaum, Binyamin. "Fed Official Says She Favors 'Prudence' in Raising Interest Rates." *New York Times*, September 12, 2016. https://www.nytimes.com/2016/09/13 /business/economy/fed-interest-rates-lael-brainard.html.

Archer, David J. "A Coming Crisis of Legitimacy?" *Sveriges Riksbank Economic Review*, no. 3 (2016): 86–95.

Arner, Douglas W., and Lotte Schou-Zibell. "Asian Regulatory Responses to the Global Financial Crisis." *Global Journal of Emerging Market Economies* 3, no. 1 (January 11, 2011): 135–69. https://doi.org/10.1177/097491011000300105.

Baker, Andrew. "Restraining Regulatory Capture? Anglo-America, Crisis Politics and Trajectories of Change in Global Financial Governance." *International Affairs* 86, no. 3 (2010): 647–63. https://doi.org/10.1111/j.1468-2346.2010.00903.x.

Baker, Colleen. "The Federal Reserve's Use of International Swap Lines." *Arizona Law Review* 55 (2013): 603–54.

Bank of Japan Act. Act No. 89 of 1997, as Amended by Act No. 102 of 2007. Japan, 2007. http://www.japaneselawtranslation.go.jp/law/detail/?id=92&vm=02&re=01.

Beckert, Jens. "Capitalism as a System of Expectations: Toward a Sociological Microfoundation of Political Economy." *Politics and Society* 41, no. 3 (September 5, 2013): 323–50. https://doi.org/10.1177/0032329213493750.

———. *Imagined Futures: Fictional Expectations and Capitalist Dynamics*. Cambridge, MA: Harvard University Press, 2016.

———. "Imagined Futures: Fictionality in Economic Action." *Theory and Society* 42, no. 3 (2013): 219–40.

Bernanke, Ben S. "'Audit the Fed' Is Not about Auditing the Fed." Brookings Institution, January 11, 2015. https://www.brookings.edu/blog/ben-bernanke/2016/01/11 /audit-the-fed-is-not-about-auditing-the-fed/.

Beunza, D. "Tools of the Trade: The Socio-technology of Arbitrage in a Wall Street Trading Room." *Industrial and Corporate Change* 13, no. 2 (April 1, 2004): 369–400. https://doi.org/10.1093/icc/dth015.

Biggart, Nicole Woolsey, and Thomas D. Beamish. "The Economic Sociology of Conventions: Habit, Custom, Practice, and Routine in Market Order." *Annual Review of Sociology* 29, no. 1 (January 1, 2003): 443–64. https://doi.org/10.1146/annurev.soc.29 .010202.100051.

Blinder, Alan S. "The Evolving Political Economy of Central Banking." Paper presented at the Changing Politics of Central Banking Conference, Cornell University, April 19, 2016. http://www.cornell.edu/video/alan-blinder-political-economy-of-cen tral-banking.

Blinder, Alan S., Charles A. E. Goodhart, Philipp M. Hildebrand, David Lipton, and Charles Wyplosz. "How Do Central Banks Talk? Geneva Reports on the World Economy No. 3." International Center for Monetary and Banking Studies, 2001. https://cepr.org/active/publications/books_reports/viewreport.php ?cvno=P147.

Buchanan, James. "The Market as a Creative Process." In *Philosophy of Economics: An Anthology*, edited by Daniel M. Hausman. Cambridge: Cambridge University Press, 1984.

Buckley, Ross P. "How East Asia Could Amplify Its Voice in Global Economic Governance." *Boston College International and Comparative Law Review* 37, no. 1 (2014): 19–51.

Bytheway, Simon James, and Mark Metzler. *Central Banks and Gold: How Tokyo, London, and New York Shaped the Modern World.* 2016.

Callon, Michel. "Introduction: The Embeddedness of Economic Markets in Economics." In *The Laws of the Markets*, edited by Michel Callon, 1–57. Oxford: Blackwell, 1998.

Canguilhem, Georges, and François Delaporte. *A Vital Rationalist: Selected Writings from Georges Canguilhem.* New York: Zone Books, 1994.

Carruthers, Bruce G., and Jeong-Chul Kim. "The Sociology of Finance." *Annual Review of Sociology* 37, no. 1 (August 11, 2011): 239–59. https://doi.org/10.1146/annurev-soc-081309-150129.

Carvalho, Fernando J. Cardim. "The Independence of Central Banks: A Critical Assessment of the Arguments." *Journal of Post Keynesian Economics* 18, no. 2 (1996): 159–75. https://doi.org/10.1080/01603477.1995.11490066.

Cohn, Carol. "Sex and Death in the Rational World of Defense Intellectuals." *Signs: Journal of Women in Culture and Society* 12, no. 4 (July 22, 1987): 687–718. https://doi.org/10.1086/494362.

Conti-Brown, Peter. *The Power and Independence of the Federal Reserve.* Princeton, NJ: Princeton University Press, 2016.

Cukierman, Alex, Steven B. Webb, and Bilin Neyapti. "Measuring the Independence of Central Banks and Its Effects on Policy Outcomes." *World Bank Economic Review* 6 (1992): 353–98. https://doi.org/10.1093/wber/6.3.353.

Desan, Christine. *Making Money: Coin, Currency, and the Coming of Capitalism.* Oxford: Oxford University Press, 2014.

Dezalay, Yves, and Bryant G. Garth. *The Internationalization of Palace Wars: Lawyers, Economists, and the Contest to Transform Latin American States.* Chicago: University of Chicago Press, 2002.

Doherty Bea, Megan. "Constructing and Maintaining Legitimacy: Sociological Perspectives of the Politics of Central Banking." Cornell University Einaudi Center Working Paper Series, Ithaca, NY, 2016. https://einaudi.cornell.edu/sites/default/files/Doherty WP 03-2016 final.pdf.

Douglas, Mary. *How Institutions Think.* Syracuse, NY: Syracuse University Press, 1986.

Drezner, Daniel W. *All Politics Is Global.* Princeton, NJ: Princeton University Press, 2008. http://www.jstor.org/stable/10.2307/j.ctt7st6p.

Farquhar, Judith. *Knowing Practice: The Clinical Encounter of Chinese Medicine.* Boulder, CO: Westview Press, 1994.

Fields, Michelle. "Sen. Cruz Cosponsors Rand Paul's 'Audit the Fed' Bill." Breitbart .com, November 12, 2015. http://www.breitbart.com/big-government/2015/11/12/sen -ted-cruz-cosponsors-rand-pauls-audit-the-fed-bill/.

Fligstein, Neil, Jonah S. Brundage, and Michael Schultz. "Seeing Like the Fed: Culture, Cognition, and Framing in the Failure to Anticipate the Financial Crisis of 2008." *American Sociological Review* 82, no. 5 (2017): 879–909. https://doi.org/10.1177 /0003122417728240.

Foucault, Michel. *The History of Sexuality.* Vol. 1, *An Introduction.* New York: Vintage, 1990.

Funke, Manuel, Moritz Schularick, and Christoph Trebesch. "Going to Extremes: Politics after Financial Crises, 1870–2014." *European Economic Review* 88 (September 2016): 227–60. https://doi.org/10.1016/j.euroecorev.2016.03.006.

Gajanan, Mahita. "Federal Reserve Chair Janet Yellen Fires Back at Donald Trump over Interest Rate." *Time*, September 21, 2016. http://time.com/4503472/janet-yellen -donald-trump-federal-reserve/.

Galeoto, Laureen E., Karen Y. Bitar, and Gil Rudolph. "The Consumer Financial Protection Bureau: The New Sheriff in Town." *Business Insights: Essentials*, September 2012, 702.

Geertz, Clifford. *The Interpretation of Cultures: Selected Essays.* New York: Basic Books, 1973.

Gilens, Martin, and Benjamin I. Page. "Testing Theories of American Politics: Elites, Interest Groups, and Average Citizens." *Perspectives on Politics* 12, no. 3 (September 18, 2014): 564–81. https://doi.org/10.1017/S1537592714001595.

Goodhart, Charles A. E. "The Constitutional Position of an Independent Central Bank." *Government and Opposition* 37, no. 2 (April 28, 2002): 190–210. https://doi.org /10.1111/1477-7053.00094.

———. "The Evolution of Central Banks," 205. Cambridge, MA: MIT Press, 1985.

Gould, J. J. "Why Is Populism Taking Over the Republican Party?" *The Atlantic*, July 2, 2016. https://www.theatlantic.com/politics/archive/2016/07/populism-ameri can-right/489800/.

Gramsci, Antonio. "The Formation of the Intellectuals." In *Selections from the Prison Notebooks of Antonio Gramsci*, edited by Quintin Hoare and Geoffrey Nowell-Smith, 483. New York: International Publishers, 1971.

Grimes, Arthur. "Monetary Policy and Economic Imbalances: An Ethnographic Examination of Central Bank Rituals." *Journal of Economic Surveys* 27, no. 4 (September 1, 2013): 634–40. https://doi.org/10.1111/joes.12024.

Gupta, Akhil, and James Ferguson. *Anthropological Locations: Boundaries and Grounds of a Field Science.* Berkeley: University of California Press, 1997.

Haan, Jakob de, and Gert Jan van 'T Hag. "Variation in Central Bank Independence across Countries: Some Provisional Empirical Evidence." *Public Choice*, 1995. https://doi.org/10.2307/30027056.

Hage, Ghassan. *Against Paranoid Nationalism: Searching for Hope in a Shrinking Society.* Annandale, NSW: Pluto Press, 2003.

Hefeker, Carsten, and Michael Neugart. "The Influence of Central Bank Transparency on Labor Market Regulation." *Manchester School* 82, no. 1 (January 2014): 17–32. https://doi.org/10.1111/j.1467-9957.2012.02334.x.

Helleiner, E., and S. Pagliari. "The End of an Era in International Financial Regulation? A Postcrisis Research Agenda." *International Organization* 65, no. 1 (2011): 169–200.

Hilgartner, Stephen. "The Dominant View of Popularization: Conceptual Problems, Political Uses." *Social Studies of Science* 20, no. 3 (August 29, 1990): 519–39. https:// doi.org/10.1177/030631290020003006.

Hogle, Linda F. "Introduction: Jurisdictions of Authority and Expertise in Science and Medicine." *Medical Anthropology* 21, nos. 3–4 (July 2002): 231–46. https://doi.org/10.1080/01459740214076.

Holmes, Douglas R. *Economy of Words: Communicative Imperatives in Central Banks.* Chicago: University of Chicago Press, 2014.

Jasanoff, Sheila. "Citizens at Risk: Cultures of Modernity in the US and EU." *Science as Culture* 11, no. 3 (2002): 363–80. https://doi.org/10.1080/0950543022000005087.

———. *Designs on Nature: Science and Democracy in Europe and the United States.* Princeton, NJ: Princeton University Press, 2005.

Jopson, Barney, and Sam Fleming. "Fed Challenged over Governor's Clinton Ties." *Financial Times*, September 28, 2016. https://www.ft.com/content/dccb1784-8599-11e6-a29c-6e7d9515ad15.

Katzenstein, Peter. "Panel: The Politics of Central Banking: What Is the State of the Art in the Social Sciences? Part I." Paper presented at the Changing Politics of Central Banking Conference, Cornell University, April 18, 2016.

Kear, Mark. "Governing Homo Subprimicus: Beyond Financial Citizenship, Exclusion, and Rights." *Antipode* 45, no. 4 (September 1, 2013): 926–46. https://doi.org/10.1111/j.1467-8330.2012.01045.x.

Kelly, C. R. R. "Financial Crisis and Civil Society." *Chicago Journal of International Law* 11, no. 2 (2011): 505–55.

Kennedy, Leonard J., Patricia A. McCoy, and Ethan Bernstein. "The Consumer Financial Protection Bureau: Financial Regulation for the Twenty-First Century." *Cornell Law Review* 97, no. 5 (2012): 1141–76.

Keynes, John Maynard. *The General Theory of Employment, Interest, and Money.* London: Macmillan, 1964.

Kingsford-Smith, Dimity, and Olivia Dixon. "The Consumer Interest and the Financial Markets." In *Oxford Handbook of Financial Regulation*, edited by Niamh Moloney, Eilís Ferran, and Jennifer Payne, 695–735. Oxford: Oxford University Press, 2015.

Kirshner, Jonathan. *Monetary Orders: Ambiguous Economics, Ubiquitous Politics.* Ithaca, NY: Cornell University Press, 2003.

Konoe, Sara. *The Politics of Financial Markets and Regulation: The United States, Japan, and Germany.* New York: Palgrave Macmillan, 2014.

Lakoff, Andrew. "From Population to Vital System: National Security and the Changing Object of Public Health." In *Biosecurity Interventions: Global Health and Security in Question*, edited by Andrew Lakoff, 33–60. New York: Columbia University Press, 2008.

Leach, Edmund R. *Custom, Law, and Terrorist Violence.* Edinburgh: University Press, 1977.

Lépinay, Vincent Antonin. *Codes of Finance: Engineering Derivatives in a Global Bank.* Princeton, NJ: Princeton University Press, 2011.

Levitin, Adam J. "The Politics of Financial Regulation and the Regulation of Financial Politics: A Review Essay." *Harvard Law Review* 127, no. 7 (May 1, 2014): 2034–63. http://go.galegroup.com/ps/i.do?p=AONE&u=nysl_sc_cornl&id=GALE%7CA368957920&v=2.1&it=r&sid=summon&authCount=1.

Levy, David A. "Does an Independent Central Bank Violate Democracy?" *Journal of Post Keynesian Economics* 18, no. 2 (1996): 189–210. https://doi.org/10.2307/4538486.

Lockwood, Erin. "The Global Politics of Central Banking: A View from Political Science." Cornell University Einaudi Center Working Paper Series, Ithaca, NY, 2016. http://www.lawschool.cornell.edu/Conferences/changing-politics-of-central-banking-conference/upload/Lockwood_2016.pdf.

MacKenzie, Donald. "An Equation and Its Worlds." *Social Studies of Science* 33, no. 6 (December 29, 2003): 831–68. https://doi.org/10.1177/0306312703336002.

Masco, Joseph. "Nuclear Technoaesthetics: Sensory Politics from Trinity to the Virtual Bomb in Los Alamos." *American Ethnologist* 31, no. 3 (2004): 349–73. https://doi.org/10.1525/ae.2004.31.3.349.

Maurer, Bill. "Resocializing Finance? Or Dressing It in Mufti?" *Journal of Cultural Economy* 1, no. 1 (2008): 65–78. https://doi.org/10.1080/17530350801913668.

McGinnis, John O. *Accelerating Democracy*. Princeton, NJ: Princeton University Press, 2012.

Mcnamara, Kathleen. "Rational Fictions: Central Bank Independence and the Social Logic of Delegation Rational Fictions; Central Bank Independence and the Social Logic of Delegation." *West European Politics* 25, no. 1 (2011): 37–41. https://doi.org/10.1080/713601585.

Metzger, Gillian E. "Through the Looking Glass to a Shared Reflection: The Evolving Relationship between Administrative Law and Financial Regulation." *Law and Contemporary Problems* 112 (2015): 129–56.

Mitchell, Timothy. *Rule of Experts: Egypt, Techno-Politics, Modernity*. Berkeley: University of California Press, 2002.

Muniesa, Fabian. "Performing Prices: The Case of Price Discovery Automation in the Financial Markets." In *Facts and Figures: Economic Representations and Practices*, edited by Hans-Jürgen Kalthoff, Herbert Rottenburg, and Richard Wagener, 289–312. Marburg: Metropolis Verlag, 2000.

Nishimura, Kiyohiko G. "Macroprudential Lessons from the Financial Crisis: A Practitioner's View." In *Asian Perspectives on Financial Sector Reforms and Regulation*, edited by Masahiro Kawai and Eswar Prasad, 180–96. Washington, DC: Asian Development Bank Institute, 2011.

Paul, Rand. "Audit the Fed." Breitbart.com, February 10, 2015. http://www.breitbart.com/big-government/2015/02/10/sen-rand-paul-audit-the-fed/.

Paul, Rand, and Mark Spitznagel. "The Fed Is Crippling America." *Time*, January 10, 2016. http://time.com/4170969/sen-rand-paul-audit-the-fed/.

Pistor, Katharina. "A Legal Theory of Finance." *Journal of Comparative Economics* 41, no. 2 (2013): 315–30.

Posen, Adam S. "Central Bank Independence after the Inflation Is Gone." Paper presented at the Changing Politics of Central Banking Conference, Cornell University, April 18, 2016. https://piie.com/system/files/documents/transcript20160418posen-cornell.pdf.

——. "Why Central Bank Independence Does Not Cause Low Inflation: There Is No Institutional Fix for Politics." Edited by Robert Marjolin and Richard O'Brien.

Finance and the International Economy 7 (1993): 41–65. https://search.proquest.com
/docview/1311988449?pq-origsite=summon.

Power, Michael, Simon Ashby, and Tommaso Palermo. *Risk Culture in Financial Organisations: A Research Report.* London, 2016. http://eprints.lse.ac.uk/67978/1/Palermo
_Rsik culture research report_2016.pdf.

Prates, Marcelo. "The Changing Politics of Central Banking: A Legal Perspective."
Cornell University Einaudi Center Working Paper Series, Ithaca, NY, 2016. http://
www.lawschool.cornell.edu/Conferences/changing-politics-of-central-banking
-conference/upload/Prates_2016.pdf.

Reuters and Fortune Editors. "Neel Kashkari Rejects Trump's Charge That the Fed Is
Beholden to Obama." *Fortune*, September 12, 2016. http://fortune.com/2016/09/12
/fed-interest-rates-kashkari/.

Riles, Annelise. *Collateral Knowledge: Legal Reasoning in the Global Financial Markets.*
Chicago: University of Chicago Press, 2011.

———. "Comparative Law and Socio-legal Studies." In *The Oxford Handbook of Comparative Law*, edited by Mathias Reimann and Reinhard Z. Zimmerman, 775–814.
Oxford: Oxford University Press, 2006.

———. "Introduction: In Response." In *Documents: Artifacts of Modern Knowledge*, edited by Annelise Riles. Ann Arbor: University of Michigan Press, 2006.

Rudnyckyj, Daromir. "Economy in Practice: Islamic Finance and the Problem of
Market Reason." *American Ethnologist* 41, no. 1 (2014): 110–27. https://doi.org/10
.1111/amet.12063.

Sanders, Bernie. "To Rein In Wall Street, Fix the Fed." *New York Times*, December 23, 2015. https://www.nytimes.com/2015/12/23/opinion/bernie-sanders-to-rein
-in-wall-street-fix-the-fed.html.

Scheurer, Jason. "The Federal Reserve Is Dealing Financial Drugs." Breitbart.com,
March 16, 2016. http://www.breitbart.com/big-government/2016/03/16/the-federal
-reserve-is-dealing-financial-drugs/.

Shelton, Judy. "Trump Is Right to Take Aim at the 'Political' Fed." *Financial Times*,
September 28, 2016. https://www.ft.com/content/c253d1b8-84cf-11e6-8897-2359a
58ac7a5.

Sismondo, Sergio. *An Introduction to Science and Technology Studies.* Malden, MA:
Wiley-Blackwell, 2010.

Sørensen, Anders Ravn. "Banking on the Nation: How Four Danish Central Bank
Governors Used and Reproduced the Logics of National Identity." *International Journal of Politics, Culture, and Society* 28, no. 4 (December 18, 2015): 325–47. https://doi
.org/10.1007/s10767-014-9196-5.

Steele, Stacey. "The Collapse of Lehman Brothers and Derivative Disputes: The Relevance of Bankruptcy Cultures to Roles for Courts and Attitudes of Judges." *Law in
Context* 30 (2014): 51–84.

Stiglitz, Joseph E. *The Euro: How a Common Currency Threatens the Future of Europe.*
New York: W. W. Norton, 2016.

Subbarao, Duvvuri. "G 20 and India." Forty-Sixth A. D Shroff Memorial Lecture, In-
dian Merchants' Chamber, Mumbai, November 20, 2012. https://www.rbi.org.in
/scripts/BS_SpeechesView.aspx?id=753.

———. *Who Moved My Interest Rate? Leading the Reserve Bank of India through Five Turbulent Years.* Gurgaon, Haryana, India: Penguin India, 2016.

Summers, Lawrence. "Here's What Bernie Sanders Gets Wrong—and Right—about the Fed." *Washington Post Wonkblog*, December 29, 2015. https://www.washingtonpost.com/news/wonk/wp/2015/12/29/larry-summers-heres-what-bernie-sanders-gets-wrong-and-right-about-the-fed/?utm_term=.3edb1974f3d9.

Tett, Gillian. *Fool's Gold: How the Bold Dream of a Small Tribe at J. P. Morgan Was Corrupted by Wall Street Greed and Unleashed a Catastrophe.* New York: Free Press, 2009.

———. "The Inflation Enigma Needs Unorthodox Answers." *Financial Times*, March 31, 2016. https://www.ft.com/content/c4137baa-f6a1-11e5-803c-d27c7117d132.

———. *The Silo Effect: The Peril of Expertise and the Promise of Breaking Down Barriers.* New York: Simon and Schuster, 2015.

Tewksbury, David, and Jason Rittenberg. *News on the Internet: Information and Citizenship in the 21st Century.* New York: Oxford University Press, 2012.

Tognato, Carlo. *Central Bank Independence: Cultural Codes and Symbolic Performance.* New York: Palgrave Macmillan, 2012.

Trachtman, Joel P. "The International Law of Financial Crisis: Spillovers, Subsidiarity, Fragmentation and Cooperation." *Journal of International Economic Law* 13, no. 3 (September 1, 2010): 719–42. https://doi.org/10.1093/jiel/jgq038.

Traweek, Sharon. *Beamtimes and Lifetimes: The World of High Energy Physicists.* Cambridge, MA: Harvard University Press, 1992.

Tsing, Anna Lowenhaupt. *Friction: An Ethnography of Global Connection.* Princeton, NJ: Princeton University Press, 2005.

Tucker, Paul. "The Credit Crisis: Lessons from a Protracted 'Peacetime.'" *Bank of England Quarterly Bulletin*, 3rd quarter (2008).

Velthuis, Olav. "Making Monetary Markets Transparent: The European Central Bank's Communication Policy and Its Interactions with the Media." *Economy and Society* 44, no. 2 (2015): 316–40. https://doi.org/10.1080/03085147.2015.1013355.

Wagner, Roy. *The Invention of Culture.* Rev. ed. Chicago: University of Chicago Press, 1981.

Warren, Elizabeth. "The New Economics of the American Family." *American Bankruptcy Institute Law Review* 12 (2004): 1–41.

Wayland, Coral. "Contextualizing the Politics of Knowledge: Physicians' Attitudes toward Medicinal Plants." *Medical Anthropology Quarterly* 17, no. 4 (2003): 483–500. https://doi.org/10.1525/maq.2003.17.4.483.

Young, Kevin L. "Transnational Regulatory Capture? An Empirical Examination of the Transnational Lobbying of the Basel Committee on Banking Supervision." *Review of International Political Economy* 19, no. 4 (2012): 663–88. https://doi.org/10.1080/09692290.2011.624976.

9 781501 732720